TRADITIONS

QUEEN MARY 2

---

the legacy continues

Cunard Line and Rolls-Royce together, what a comforting thought.

The name Cunard Line has always been synonymous with peerless cruising but perhaps the Rolls-Royce association is less well known. While you may be aware that our world-leading technology plays a major role in the skies, it is comforting to know that our propulsion and stabilisation equipment helps this magnificent vessel to cruise so serenely. So as you relax and enjoy the splendour of your cruise, we are proud to join with Cunard Line to ensure you have the smoothest of voyages and that your martini is served stirred and not shaken. **Trusted to deliver excellence**

www.rolls-royce.com

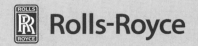

FRETTE

Milan Rome Venice Capri Paris London Marbella Moscow
New York Aspen Beverly Hills Chicago San Francisco South Coast Plaza Tokyo

FIN·PART www.frette.com

We also fly for fun.

We take your fun seriously. After all, you've worked hard for your time off. So treat yourself. Go someplace exotic. Or visit family and friends. Just call US Airways® at 1-800-428-4322, 1-800-622-1015 for international reservations, or contact your travel agent. Or go to **usairways.com**.

 **U·S AIRWAYS**

usairways.com

Winston Churchill
Reid's Palace 1950

George Bernard Shaw
Reid's Palace 1924

On a cliff-top headland overlooking the Bay of Funchal, Reid's Palace in Madeira is surrounded by a 10-acre paradise of sub-tropical gardens. Madeira enjoys a wonderful, mild year-round climate, making it the ideal location for outdoor leisure pursuits, such as watersports and golf, or simply basking in the sunshine and gazing across the deep blue of the Atlantic Ocean.

In 1891, the Reid family opened the doors of their new hotel and ushered in a new era of elegance. The hotel combines grand Edwardian tradition with all of the amenities and comforts to be expected from a modern, luxury property, and has attracted many exalted guests over the years, including George Bernard Shaw, Winston Churchill and John Huston.

Perfect for invigoration or revitalisation, challenging activity or relaxed breaks, it is the ideal rendezvous, combining refined luxury with discreet service and superb cuisine.

Reid's Palace
Pleasures Past & Present

The dining room
Reid's Palace

Afternoon tea on the terrace
Reid's Palace

For reservations or further information, please call our representative office in the US, Crown International, on +1 201 265 51 51 or toll free in the UK on 0800 092 1723.

Reid's Palace, P-9000-098, Funchal, Madeira, Portugal. Tel: +351 291 71 7171; fax: +351 291 71 7177; email: reservations@reidspalace.com

www.reidspalace.orient-express.com

ORIENT-EXPRESS
HOTELS
A member of
The Leading Hotels of the World

We knew our Upper Class would have competition someday.

We never dreamed it would be from a ship.

IMAGINE AN ISLAND

Holidays in Gran Canaria are more than just days of rest. You discover part of yourself.

Clean beaches of golden sand. Palm oasis.
Centuries old pine forest and deep ravines.
Cities and towns with more than 500 years of history.
And where you can also practice windsurf, golf, horse-riding,
scuba diving, mountain biking, surfing, parachuting,
deep - sea fishing, mountaineering...

Canary Islands

GRAN CANARIA

Cabildo de
Gran Canaria

www.grancanaria.com

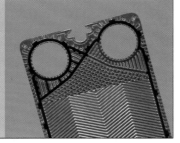

Bill Panoff	*Publisher*
Linda Douthat	*Associate Publisher/Creative Director*
Jeffrey Laign	*Editorial Director*
Jodi Ornstein	*Managing Editor*
James P. Karpinen • Laura Roche	*Art Direction*
Catherine Rowe	*Designer*
Andrea Klee	*Proofreader*
Gary Buchanan, Abby Ellin, Matt Hannafin, Susan Pierres, Simon Veness	*Contributing Writers*
Harvey Lloyd	*Contributing Photographer*
Maria Baro	*Production Manager*
Tammy Robinson	*Assistant Production Manager*
Paola Gomez	*Creative Assistant*

The publisher wishes to thank Edie Bornstein, Linda Schultes, Julie Davis, and their team for their tireless efforts in the production of this commemorative book.

The QM2 Commemorative Book is published under contract to The PPI Group, 4517 NW 31st Avenue, Fort Lauderdale, Florida 33309-3403. Phone: 954-377-7777 • Fax: 954-377-7000 E-mail: bpanoff@ppigroup.com • Web site: www.ppigroup.com

Daniel Rose, Alan McCarthy, Kieran Gannon, Chris England	*Advertising Sales*

Bill Panoff	*President/Chief Executive Officer*
Irene Panoff	*Chief Operations Officer*
Jose I. Martin	*Chief Financial Officer*
Linda Douthat	*Vice President, Publishing*
Mitch Pizik	*Vice President, Sales & Marketing*
Pepe Fernandez	*Vice President, Information Technologies*
Joe McGrath	*Vice President, Onboard Marketing*
Jeffrey Laign	*Editorial Director*
Tony Scarpa	*Controller*
J.D. Andrews	*Director of Broadcast Operations*

▶ **NEVER**
LOSES HER
EDGE

SASHA COHEN, International figure skater

NEVER ◀
NEEDS A
BATTERY

CITIZEN
ECO-DRIVE

The most famous ocean liners in the world and one of the world's leading watch manufacturers have combined to create the Limited Edition Citizen QM2 Watch.

Available exclusively onboard in Ladies' and Gents variations, the Ladies' features 38 diamonds.

Each stunning watch is individually numbered and presented in a luxury QM2 inscribed wooden box.

▶ **SIMPLY UNSTOPPABLE**

Aruba | Only the Best!

A Dutch multilingual Caribbean island, rich in history and culture, Aruba offers you unique experiences… everything you'll need to enjoy a vacation to cherish forever: miles of white sandy beaches, exhilarating watersports, professional golf and tennis, horseback riding, sightseeing tours, exquisite dining, dazzling casinos, exciting nightlife and fabulous shopping.

contributors

Abby Ellin

Matt Hannafin

Susan Pierres

Simon Veness

Abby Ellin writes the "Preludes" column about young people and money in the Sunday Money & Business section of *The New York Times*. She has traveled extensively around the world and is the former travel editor for *Hamptons Magazine*. Her work has been published in a number of magazines and newspapers, including *Time*, *Spy*, *Salon*, *Maxim*, *Mademoiselle*, *Marie Claire*, and *The New York Times Magazine*. She lives in New York City.

Matt Hannafin is the cruise editor at *Frommer's Travel Guides*, a regular writer for the travel trade newspaper *Travel Weekly*, and a contributor to such diverse publications as the *Boston Herald* and Jim Crotty and Michael Lane's irreverent *Mad Monks' Guide to New York City* (Macmillan Travel, 1999). In his spare time, Matt is a performing percussionist specializing in Persian classical and folk music. He lives in New York City.

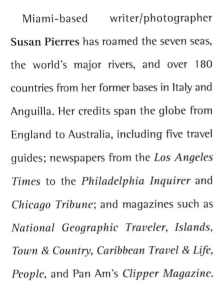

Miami-based writer/photographer **Susan Pierres** has roamed the seven seas, the world's major rivers, and over 180 countries from her former bases in Italy and Anguilla. Her credits span the globe from England to Australia, including five travel guides; newspapers from the *Los Angeles Times* to the *Philadelphia Inquirer* and *Chicago Tribune*; and magazines such as *National Geographic Traveler*, *Islands*, *Town & Country*, *Caribbean Travel & Life*, *People*, and Pan Am's *Clipper Magazine*.

Simon Veness is a journalist and travel writer who has pioneered the development of the best-selling *Brit's Guide* travel book series. At 39 going on 99, Simon also contributes to newspapers such as *The Times* and *The Sun*. He is also coordinator of the British Cruise Awards, editor of *World Cruising* magazine, and a sports sub-editor with *The Sun*. Married with two young children, he chooses to travel in his spare time, preferably by ship.

Announcing a new Orient-Express experience
HOTEL RITZ

Ranked amongst the top ten hotels in the world and set in the cultural heart of the Spanish capital, the prestigious Hotel Ritz is close to the Prado and Thyssen museums. A haunt of European royalty since its opening in 1910, the hotel is also popular with Spain's political and show business elites, attracted by its exemplary standards of quality and service, which have earned the Ritz an unrivalled prestige.

For reservations or further information, please contact our representaive office in the US, Crown International, on +1 201 265 51 51 or toll free number in the UK on 0800 092 1723. Ritz Madrid, Plaza de la Lealtad 5, 28014 Madrid, Spain, Tel: +34 91 701 67 67; fax: +34 91 701 67 76; e-mail: comercial@ritz.es or www.ritzmadrid.com

ORIENT-EXPRESS
HOTELS

www.orient-express.com

A member of
The Leading Hotels of the World

Above: *The Terrace and Gardens at the Hotel Ritz provide the perfect meeting place in Madrid for a delightful "al fresco" lunch, dinner or typical Spanish tapas dining.*

table of contents

Sidecar document case. Super 130's wool suit. At 21 old bond street.
selfridges. 48 jermyn street. royal exchange. www.dunhill.com

Everything but the motor

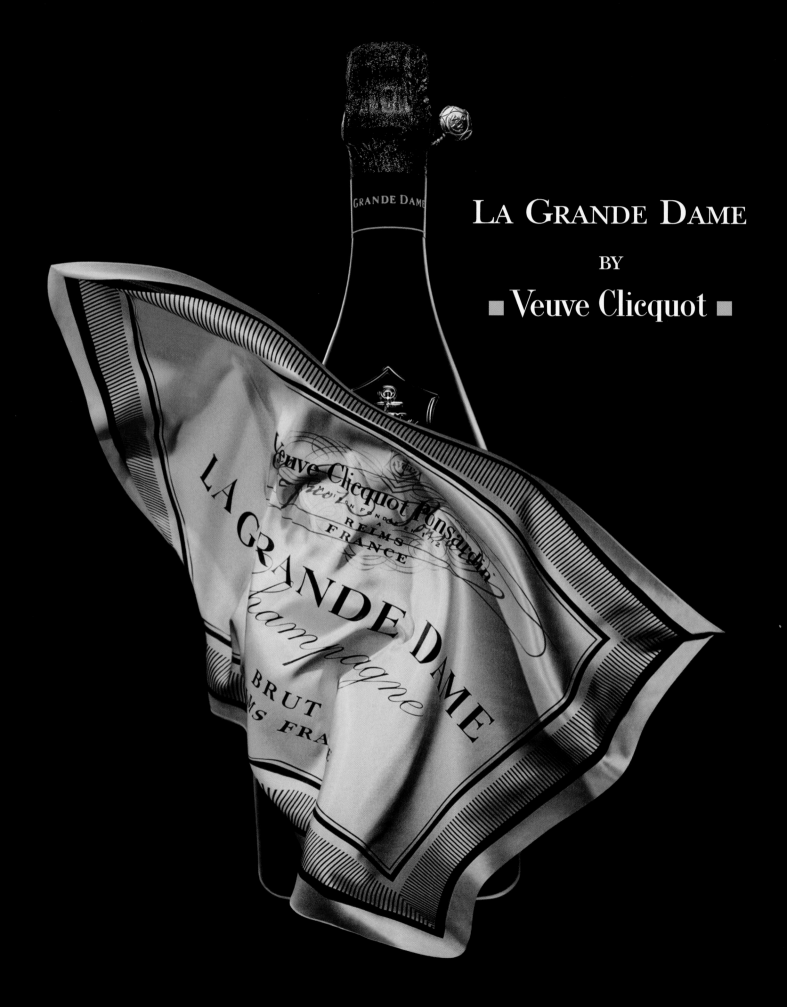

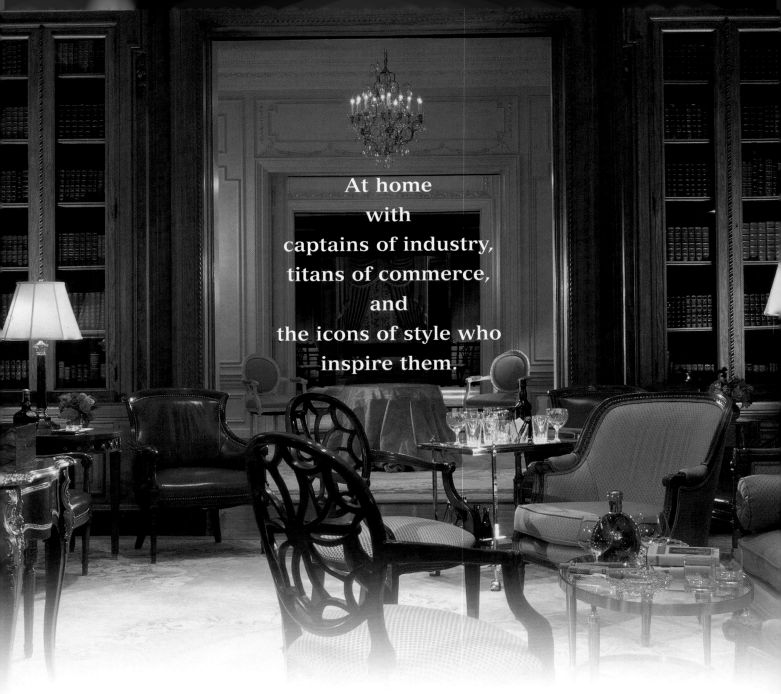

From Superyacht to Superliner

Whatever the size of your vessel, MANTA, the world-leading integrated bridge system from Kelvin Hughes, can be tailored to your bridge environment.

Marking another milestone in the ongoing programme of product innovation and development at Kelvin Hughes, such is the quality of MANTA that Cunard has specified it for installation on its QM2 flagship. But MANTA's modular concept, sophisticated design and advanced ergonomics make it ideally suited not only superliners, but also to superyachts and other kinds of vessel.

MANTA from Kelvin Hughes – at the forefront of navigational technology.

KELVIN HUGHES

UK (Head Office): Kelvin Hughes Limited
Telephone: +44 20 8500 1020
Benelux: Kelvin Hughes (Nederland) bv
Telephone: +31 10 416 76 22
China: Kelvin Hughes Shanghai Representative Office
Telephone: +86 21 58772105
Far East: Kelvin Hughes (Singapore) Pte Ltd
Telephone: +65 6545 9880
Scandinavia: A/S Kelvin Hughes
Telephone: +45 86 11 28 88

www.kelvinhughes.com

smiths
A part of Smiths Marine Systems

Take a sip of the ocean

H$_2$O.

More than three quarters of our planet is covered by water. Unfortunately, 97.5% of it is salty. So, ironically, about 500 million people living in coastal areas don't have enough water to drink.

Desalination of seawater is therefore a very important process. And not just on land, but also on board ships to ensure that crew and passengers have reliable access to fresh water. Alfa Laval is a well-known brand at sea. More than three quarters of all ships currently in operation use our equipment for fresh water production, cleaning of fuel, lubrication of oil and engine cooling.

Pure Performance: Water. Oil. Chemicals. Beverages. Foodstuffs. Starch. Pharmaceuticals. You name it. Alfa Laval is helping most types of industries to refine and improve their products and to optimize the performance of their processes. Time and time again.

Our equipment, systems and service are hard at work in more than 100 countries, and across the seven seas. Helping to create better living conditions for mankind everywhere.

www.alfalaval.com

It feels even better when you buy tax free.

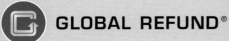 **GLOBAL REFUND**®   **Over 22,000 satisfied customers every day.**

There's so much to see in America, you'll need a great place to relax.

Sheraton New York Hotel & Towers, New York

Sheraton New York Hotel & Towers, New York

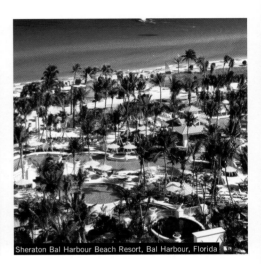
Sheraton Bal Harbour Beach Resort, Bal Harbour, Florida

See America. Stay with us.

WESTIN
HOTELS & RESORTS

Sheraton
HOTELS & RESORTS

Four Points
Sheraton

ST. REGIS

THE LUXURY COLLECTION

W
HOTELS

the legacy

"So is this great and wide sea, wherein are things creeping innumerable, both small and great beast.

There go the ships; there is that leviathan, whom thou hast made to play therein."

–Psalms 104:19-27

the institution

Queen Mary, New York

what's in a name? why call the new ship *Queen Mary 2?*
In Cunard Line's illustrious fleet are many famous names.

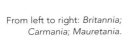
From left to right: *Britannia;*
Carmania; Mauretania.

How about *Britannia*, after the ship that started it all for Cunard more than a century and a half ago? Like the *Queen Mary 2*, *Britannia* was an industry leader. When she debuted in 1840, *Britannia* amazed the world with her radically bold design. The magnificent ocean greyhound perfectly embodied the far-reaching vision of line founder Samuel Cunard, who imbued her with his grand dreams and sense of purpose.

Britannia went on to carve out a unique niche in the annals of maritime history. Her name, in fact, long ruled the waves. *Britannia*, remember, was the name of Queen Elizabeth II's royal yacht. Until she was decommissioned in 1997, that majestic vessel served Her Majesty well as a nautical ambassador.

Britannia's association with royalty qualified the name as a contender for Cunard's new liner. After all, the staff and crew of *QM2* make every effort to ensure

that all passengers are treated like royalty. But *Queen Mary 2* is more than gracious. She also is a trail blazer, a showpiece for the grandest technological innovations. In that sense, she resembles her older sister, *Carmania*.

It was in 1905 that Cunard launched the first ship to bear that name. *Carmania*'s achievements were legion. She was, for example, the first ship to be fitted with steam turbines, an advance that paved the way for the high-tech pod propulsion system that is a notable feature of *QM2*. *Carmania*'s brilliant engineering heralded a bold new design phase at Cunard. *Carmania*, in fact, reclaimed the coveted Blue Riband award for the fastest transatlantic crossing.

Mauretania took technology even further. Launched in 1907, she benefited enormously from rapidly developing steam turbine technology and held the Blue Riband for 22 years. Because of

Mauretania's record of distinguished service and her reputation for supreme style, Cunard might well have considered reviving the name in 2003.

Carinthia would have been another option. Dating from 1925, she was built in the great traditions of the North Atlantic trade. What's more, *Carinthia* gave the cruise industry a glimpse of things to come. For the first time, a ship was offering most of its accommodation to tourists, not just to wealthy passengers. Extremely popular with the public, *Carinthia* was a beloved servant of the Cunard fleet whose name is remembered fondly.

There would have been merit as well in considering *Queen Elizabeth 3* as a name for the new liner. The *QE2* made headlines the world over when she first graced the seas in 1969.

So why *Queen Mary 2*? To understand the reasoning behind Cunard's choice of names, let's turn back the clock to 1936, the year the original *Queen Mary* made herself known to the world.

Elegance and Optimism

The first *Queen Mary* was like nothing the cruise industry had seen before. She embodied elegance and optimism in her design, welcome concepts in

From left to right: Maiden voyage of *Carinthia III*; The launch of *Queen Elizabeth 2*; Deck games on *Queen Mary*.

that troubled era of political and economic uncertainty. The liner bespoke innovation and achievement, glamour and charisma, unsurpassed graciousness. That she lives today as a hotel in Long Beach, California, is a tribute to her timeless quality.

When *Queen Mary* plied the seas, cruise lines considered transatlantic voyages their most important routes. As such, lines looked for the biggest, boldest ships to attract cruisers with panache. Turning out the biggest and best liners was the key to competing for passengers, cargo, and the Blue Riband. Soon such magnificent vessels came to symbolize entire generations and reflect national pride.

When the original *Queen Mary* entered service on a sunny day in May, the public spotlight burned intensely. She made her mark from the start and proved beyond a doubt that she could meet the expectations of an age – and then some. Throughout her illustrious life, she racked up achievement after achievement. Her grand sense of style never left her, even when she cloaked herself in wartime gray and transformed herself into the best troopship ever seen.

The queen of the seas was a favourite of celebrities, from royalty to stars, and she offered a classic ambiance to all who sailed with her. Her marriage of technological and aesthetic qualities endeared her to countless passengers.

Now Cunard has revived her simple but elegant name in a new age. It is an immense challenge for the designers and builders of this new age to live up to such a legacy of supreme and illustrious quality. Without a doubt, *QM2* will make her predecessor proud.

Why *Queen Mary 2*? It is a fundamental name, a gracious name – the perfect name for the perfect ship.

the tradition

The maiden voyage of *Queen Mary*, 1936, New York Harbor

Queen Mary 2 is heir to the grand legacy
left by her legendary sister ships.

From its humble beginnings more than a century and a half ago, Cunard Line went on to dominate transatlantic cruising, offering passengers gracious service unparalleled in the industry.

The long, proud tradition of the most famous name in maritime history dates back to 1839 when Samuel Cunard won the contract from the British Admiralty to operate a monthly North Atlantic mail service. The enterprising Canadian promptly formed the British and North American Royal Mail Steam Packet Company to ferry mail from the United Kingdom to Canada and the United States. But there was more than mail to Cunard's vision. In no time, Cunard was taking on passengers.

On July 4, 1840, the company's first transatlantic passenger steamship, *Britannia*, sailed from Liverpool for Halifax and Boston. Just two decks high, this 1,154-ton, Clyde-built, wooden paddle-steamer had a maximum speed of just 8.5 knots. The Royal Mail was the principal cargo, but 63 passengers and 93 crewmembers also were on board for the journey, which took a little more than 14 days. Conditions on the ship were spartan, but the ship's cow provided the luxury of fresh milk.

In 1856, the company's first iron-hulled ship, *Persia*, took the prestigious Blue Riband award for the fastest Atlantic crossing. Six years later, *China*, Cunard's first screw-propelled North Atlantic liner, had the distinction of being the first Cunarder offering immigrant accommodation to America.

Cunard's industry dominance was challenged in 1870 by the advent of White Star Line's *Oceanic*, a 17,000-tonne behemoth that one industry analyst described as, "the ship which makes possible the concept of a steamship as a traveling palace."

Cunard had to catch up if it wanted to maintain its position. A year later, the company introduced the steel-hulled *Servia*, the first express liner designed to rely solely on passenger revenue. Capable of achieving 17 knots, *Servia* was made for fast passages. Thus was born the era of the Ocean Greyhound.

But Cunard ships weren't just fast. The line was earning a solid reputation for elegance and fine service. *Aurania*, which catered exclusively to wealthy cruisers, entered the market in 1883, boasting amenities such as spacious suites with marble bathrooms. The following year, *Etruria* and *Umbria*, the first Cunarders to outclass their rivals in size and capacity, entered service.

In 1893 the first twin-screw liners, *Campania* and *Lucania* – each 12,950 tonnes – were record breakers from the outset. Their service speed of 21 knots made them the fastest ships on the North Atlantic route. Cunard saw another memorable year in 1907, when the four-funnelled, 31,500-tonne express liners *Lusitania* and *Mauretania* became the first "Grand Hotels" at sea, complete with Palm Courts, à la carte restaurants, electric lifts, and telephones. What's more, they had a service speed of 24 knots. *Mauretania*'s maiden crossing of the Atlantic took just four days, 22 hours and 29 minutes.

Now that Cunard maintained supremacy on the Liverpool-to-New York route, the line turned its attention to the Boston service. In 1911 and 1912, Cunard introduced a new concept with the 18,000-tonne *Franconia* and *Laconia*. The ships were designed to undertake winter cruises out of New York to the Mediterranean as well as line voyages.

A New Era

Then World War 1 changed the face of cruising. The 1915 sinking of

From left to right: Lounge aboard *Aurania III*; *Franconia II*; Dining aboard *Lusitania*; Loading *Lusitania*; Ticket for *Etruria*.

Cunard's *Lusitania* brought the United States into the conflict. By the armistice signing in 1918, Cunard had lost no fewer than 22 ships – 56 percent of its pre-war tonnage.

But Cunard emerged from the conflagration in a healthier position than many of her competitors. In 1922, *Laconia* embarked on the first world cruise. By 1925, the line had taken delivery of 13 new ships, which sailed along with the refurbished *Mauretania* and *Aquitania*, sailing from Southampton to New York. It was a time of indulgence – the Roaring '20s – but the fun would not last. The Great Depression was just around the corner.

Undaunted by downturns, Cunard placed an order with the John Brown shipyard in Clydebank, Scotland, for a vessel to replace *Mauretania*. It was to be of revolutionary design, the 148th Cunard liner to be put into ocean-going service in 98 years. In December 1930, workers laid the keel of the then-unnamed titan.

But the following year, as the world economic climate worsened, Cunard suspended work on the leviathan. Then a new plan developed. The British Treasury agreed to finance completion of the liner and a sister ship if Cunard would take over White Star Line's Atlantic operation.

From left to right: *Mauretania*; Gents Lounge aboard *Laconia II*; Troops during World War II aboard *Queen Mary*.

Thus, Cunard White Star Line came into being in 1934.

Two years later, on May 27, 1936, Cunard's groundbreaking *Queen Mary* sailed on her maiden voyage to New York. Later the same year, Cunard laid the keel on *Queen Mary*'s running mate in the same shipyard. On Sept. 27, 1938, the vessel was named *Queen Elizabeth*.

But before she could be fitted out, Europe once again was plunged into conflict. World War II took great toll on Cunard, which lost 17 of its ships, including *Lancastria*.

Cunard did its part to aid the Allied cause, converting *Queen Mary* and *Queen Elizabeth* to troop ships. In his memoirs, Sir Winston Churchill said that the two Atlantic "Queens" had been instrumental in shortening the war by at least a year.

In 1949, the second Cunarder to bear the name *Caronia* entered North Atlantic service. In size and speed she was a consort to *Mauretania* of 1939, but this famous Cunarder is remembered as the first vessel built by the line dedicated to the pursuit of cruising.

From her maiden voyage in January 1949, *Caronia* was a showstopper. Known as the "Green Goddess" – her hull was four shades of green – she was fully air-conditioned, and every cabin boasted a private bathroom.

To any self-respecting globetrotter, "Going Cunard" was the ultimate cachet. But the advent of air travel cut into the North Atlantic cruising route; the days of the "Atlantic Ferry Deluxe" were numbered. In the final decades of the 20th century, many believed that the *belle époque* of the great ocean liners

was finally over. But industry observers failed to take into account the tenacity and the inventiveness of the heirs of Samuel Cunard.

Queen Mary arrived in Southampton for the last time on September 27, 1967; *Queen Elizabeth* was retired the following year. By this time, the hull of a new "*Queen*" was taking shape in the same shipyard that had created her predecessors. This was to be a scion that was quite simply the most powerful, most elegant, most advanced merchant ship afloat. On May 2, 1969, *Queen Elizabeth 2* entered service.

Now *Queen Mary 2* sets sail for Cunard. Gracious, elegant, luxurious, the new liner will make her mark in the annals of cruising history as she carries on in the grand tradition of her sisters.

the first

The Queen Mary, Long Beach, CA

Maiden Voyage, New York, *Queen Mary*; First-class dining room aboard *Queen Mary*.

the majestic *Queen Mary* – the new *QM2*'s predecessor –
epitomized grace and elegance in travel.

From left to right: The launch of *Queen Mary*, 1934; *Queen Mary* transporting troops during World War II; *Queen Mary* at open sea; the Statue of Liberty greets *Queen Mary* into New York's harbor.

On September 30, 1934, His Majesty King George V addressed 200,000 cheering spectators who had gathered at the John Brown Shipyard at Clydebank in Scotland. Towering above the spectators was the massive hull of Cunard Line's Job Number 534.

For months, speculation had run wild concerning the new ship's name. Then the king's beloved Queen Mary stepped up to the microphone. "I am happy to name this ship *Queen Mary*," she told the crowd. It was the first time in history that a merchant vessel bore the name of a member of the British royal family and the first time that the public had heard the broadcasted voice of a monarch. Her Majesty then cut a ribbon that released a bottle of Australian wine, which smashed across the liner's colossal bow. As the enormous steel hull slid down the ways into the River Clyde, she was the ultimate proof that Britannia still ruled the waves.

From the outset, *Queen Mary* was a ship of superlatives. She was the first British ship longer than 1,000 feet (1,019 feet, six inches); her displacement registered 80,773 tonnes, and she could hold 776 passengers in Cabin Class, 784 in Tourist Class, and 579 in Third Class. In addition, *Queen Mary* boasted 38 public rooms, including 13 bars. Towering 14 decks high, this city at sea was the epitome of elegant travel. She became for the world the supreme symbol of majesty and luxury.

Queen Mary arrived at the North River pier in New York on June 1, 1936, escorted by hundreds of small craft, circling aircraft, and Moran tenders spouting water. President Franklin D. Roosevelt led the welcoming committee.

Three months later, the pride of the Cunard fleet steamed across the Atlantic from Bishop's Rock to Ambrose in four days, 27 minutes, at an average speed of

30.14 knots; she made the return trip in three days, 23 hours, 57 minutes, at 30.63 knots. The "Atlantic Greyhound" was the first to accomplish a crossing in less than four days. After a few exchanges of the prestigious Blue Riband with the French Line's *Normandie*, *Queen Mary* secured the award in August 1938, after making the 2,938-nautical-mile crossing at an average speed of 31.69 knots.

In September 1939, when World War II began, *Queen Mary* was laid up in New York, but her potential as a troop ship was undeniable. The Ministry of Shipping requisitioned the grand liner for war duty, replacing her striking reds and blacks with wartime gray. Joining *Queen Mary* in New York on March 7, 1940, was *Queen Elizabeth*, already painted a leaden hue. The two "Gray Ghosts" were berthed alongside *Normandie*. It was the first and last time the three largest liners in the world would meet.

During the war, the *Queens* carried more than 1.6 million troops across more than a million nautical miles. Adolf Hitler offered $250,000 and a medal to any U-boat commander who could sink them. But the *Queens'* speed and ability to steer a zigzag course were no match for the Reich.

Shortly after the war, the *Queens* were decommissioned and refurbished. In July 1947, they resumed transatlantic service. With weekly departures in each direction, *Queen Elizabeth* and *Queen Mary* became the most commercially successful pair of ships ever built. To paraphrase a contemporary Cunard advertisement, "Getting There Wasn't Just Half the Fun – It was the Fun."

But in the 1950s, grace gave way to pace. As airlines grew, demand for ship crossings began to dwindle. The last time that more passengers crossed the North Atlantic by sea than by air was 1958. By 1961, passenger numbers were down even more.

Final Days

In 1963, Cunard decided to deploy *Queen Elizabeth* and *Queen Mary* as cruise ships. Their ability to take on the job was hampered by their inability to traverse the Panama or Suez canals as well as their lack of air-conditioning. This last-ditch measure was not a success. Cunard finally decided to retire *Queen Mary* from service after the 1967 summer season; *Queen Elizabeth* took her leave in October of the following year.

During her 33 years of service, *Queen Mary* – the last of the three-funnelled ships – amassed an amazing record of achievements including 1,001 transatlantic crossings. She steamed nearly 3.8 million nautical miles and carried more than 2 million passengers.

Queen Mary's final voyage was scheduled for October 31, 1967. Billed as the "Last Great Cruise," the voyage would be remarkable. The 14,559-mile route would take 40 days and the ship would visit Lisbon, Las Palmas, Rio de Janeiro, Valparaiso, Callao, Balboa, and Acapulco. It would also be the first time a Cunard *Queen* had navigated Cape Horn.

Queen Mary, flying her 310-foot-long "paying off" pennant (10 feet for each of her 31 years service), sailed from

From left to right: *Queen Elizabeth* and *Queen Mary* in New York; Pool aboard *Queen Mary*.

Queen Mary Public Relations

Southampton for the final time with 1,093 passengers and 806 crewmembers. The Band of the Royal Marines played "Auld Lang Syne" and coloured streamers waved from the Promenade Deck. As *Queen Mary* passed the row of dock cranes, each nodded, one-by-one, in salute, and 14 Royal Navy helicopters, in an anchor formation, flew overhead.

But *Queen Mary*'s story was far from finished. Long Beach, California, had bought her at auction for $3.45 million and had big plans to turn her into a tourist attraction and hotel.

When she arrived in Long Beach on December 9, the former Cunarder was greeted by a flotilla of more than 10,000 small craft and yachts, as thousands of onlookers crowded the shore. A DC9 jet dropped carnations on the ship's upper decks, re-creating the welcome she received in New York on her maiden voyage 31 years earlier. On the bridge,

Captain John Treasure Jones ordered "Finished with engines" at 12:07 p.m., signaling the end of the leviathan's maritime career.

As Long Beach's principal attraction, *Queen Mary* opened in May 1971 in a specially constructed lagoon. Some observers were dismayed to see this maritime legend as a tourist attraction; others were delighted that she had been saved for future generations.

The accommodation offered at the Hotel Queen Mary are much as they were when cruisers sailed the sea. The ambiance is remarkable in Main Deck or Upper Deck staterooms. Sturdy walnut furniture and Art Deco trimmings, not to mention the bakelite air vents and cast-iron portholes, transport guests back in time to a grander, gentler era – an era defined by the grand and gentle *Queen Mary*, Queen of the Sea.

the family tree

descended from the great "Queens of Atlantic,"
QM2 enjoys a lineage as unique as it is illustrious.

From left to right: Royal visit, Queen Mother aboard *Queen Elizabeth*, 1948; *QE2*'s Caronia Restaurant.

For more than 160 years, Cunard has been synonymous with tradition. At this legendary line, the past is never forgotten. Indeed, Cunard builds its ships by blending the best attributes of former vessels with the latest innovations. The result is a family tree more resplendent than any other in the maritime world.

Nowhere is tradition more prevalent than in the naming of ships. For decades all ships in the line were given names ending in "ia," a tradition started in 1840 by *Britannia*, the first name in the Cunard family tree.

But in 1934, when Cunard began building Job Number 534, the line determined that it would be more fitting to name such a majestic vessel after a monarch.

According to several accounts, Cunard had decided upon Queen Victoria, in honour of Britain's most beloved queen, who reigned for 62 years until her death in 1901. Queen Victoria's reign not only was the longest but the most glorious in English history.

Two Cunard officers, Sir Percy Bates and Sir Ashley Sparks, were sent to make the royal request of King George V. "Your Majesty," Sir Ashley announced, "we are pleased to inform you that Cunard wishes your approval to name our newest and greatest liner after England's greatest queen (King George V's grandmother)."

The king misunderstood (perhaps deliberately) and replied, "My wife will be delighted." His wife? Queen Mary, of course. And so Cunard named its ship.

This wasn't the only time there would be confusion over names of ships in Cunard's famous family tree. Consider *Queen Elizabeth 2*. Did the name bestowed by Elizabeth II in September 1967 refer to Her Majesty, or was it simply the second liner to bear the name *Queen Elizabeth*?

The ship, Cunard officials explained, was the second liner to bear the name. But confusion remains to this day. Some writers still incorrectly employ the sovereign's Roman numeral instead of the ship's number. A reference to Queen Elizabeth II, Cunard points out, is to the monarch, not the vessel. Harry Smith, *QE2*'s former assistant purser, understood that better than most. In 1969, he received a letter addressed to 'The QE II.' Smith promptly returned it to the Post Office with a note: "Try Buckingham Palace."

Family Resemblance

The second Cunard liner to bear the name *Queen Mary* will maintain many of the great traditions that have made the family tree famous in merchant shipping – but there will be some differences.

The original *Queen Mary* prided herself on crossing the Atlantic at record speeds. The majestic three-stacker won many prizes, including the Hale Trophy and Blue Riband. *Queen Mary 2* will never cross the Atlantic at record-breaking speeds. For today's transatlantic queen, the emphasis is on style, not speed.

Of course, *QM2*, like her older sisters, will cross the ocean. But she will take a course south of the "Great Circle" route followed by her predecessors. And, like the first *Queen Mary*, you'll hear the new *QM2* from miles away. The legendary *Queen Mary*'s whistle, a resonant blast at two octaves below Middle C, was audible for 10 miles. Cunard has converted the original whistle from steam to compressed air and mounted it on *QM2*'s funnel.

Accommodation on *Queen Mary 2* also reflect the family's sense of style and grace – with some differences. There were class distinctions on the original

Queen Mary. Cabin Class was considered most prestigious; its passengers never mingled with those in Tourist Class, and they, in turn, did not set foot in Third Class quarters.

In keeping with the times, *QM2* is far more egalitarian. All passengers are accorded the same gracious style and service. The new ship, though, does offer 25 grades of accommodation, ranging from spacious and elegant to ultra-luxurious.

Family traditions apply not only to ships in the Cunard fleet, but also to those who guide them. In 1969, the first captain of *QE2* was Commodore William Warwick. Thirty-four years later, the man in command of the new *QM2* is his son, Captain Ronald W. Warwick, who also followed in his father's footsteps as Master of *QE2* from 1990 to 2003.

Now Warwick is carrying on a family tradition, as is the ship he commands. The original *Queen Mary* was the result of the most complex integration of design and machinery ever attempted. Her younger sister, *QM2*, is keeping that tradition alive, while bringing new accolades to Cunard's prestigious family tree.

Micky Arison and
Captain Ronald W. Warwick

©Harvey Lloyd

Forever Elegant

The *Queen Mary 2* combines the grandeur of the past with the most up-to-date safety features

the heritage

following in his father's footsteps, Captain Ronald W. Warwick takes the helm of Cunard's newest ship, *Queen Mary 2*.

The long, storied history of Cunard Line is illuminated with the names of many who have commanded fabled ships: Commodore Ridley, who manned *Britannia*, Cunard's first transatlantic steamer; Captain Arthur Rostron, at the helm of *Carpathia*, as she charged to the rescue of *Titanic* survivors; Captain J. Treasure Jones, whose original *Queen Mary* came to epitomise maritime style and grace.

The story behind the man who guides the new *Queen Mary 2* is every bit as fascinating as those of his predecessors. Captain Ronald W. Warwick, a veteran of six ships in the Cunard fleet, brings to the new liner some 45 years of nautical experience, 33 of them in the service of Cunard.

Warwick's maritime achievements easily could fill a book. He worked his way up from a junior officer to the highest command, sailed aboard *Queen Elizabeth 2* during the Falklands War, and served as a Lieutenant Commander in the British Royal Navy Reserve, all the while collecting a cornucopia of awards and honours.

But Warwick's unique family legacy is as captivating as his curriculum vitae. His father, Commodore William Warwick, was first to command QE2 in 1969. Following in his father's footsteps, Ron Warwick later took the helm of that classic liner and now is first to command QM2.

"I started out in cargo ships and only got involved with the passenger-ship side of the trade in the 1970s," Warwick says from his country cottage in rural Somerset, England. "It didn't take long to realize that the future for passenger ships wasn't that buoyant."

The burgeoning airline industry was making major inroads in the transatlantic ship trade and many lines had to struggle

to stay afloat. "If you had asked me, perhaps as late as 1998, if there would ever be a replacement for *QE2* I would have said no. Then, when Carnival Corporation took over Cunard and announced they were to do another Queen liner, it was just incredible."

A New Chapter

Warwick says, "Cunard was well aware of the family history, so they asked me if I would be interested in being captain of *QM2*. I think my response was fairly positive!"

And why not? The sea, after all, is in Warwick's blood. He knew that as a child, but it wasn't until he was grown that the fact hit home.

"Of course, I was aware that my father was an officer and then a captain in the famous Cunard Line," he says, "but it was only when I went to sea myself that I could fully appreciate what his position was."

The younger Warwick started out in the shipping trade. "I was chief officer of the *MV Jamaica Planter*," he recalls. "We were plying between Jamaica and England on the banana trade. I enjoyed Jamaica, the ship, and the work and had no great intentions of changing things."

Then one day *QE2*, which his father commanded, anchored in Kingston and Ron Warwick decided to pay him a visit. He was, he says, "overwhelmed" by the ship and its technological marvels – not to mention his father's prowess as commander.

"It was then that I realised that to be a captain of a passenger liner, especially a Cunard liner, was very special. I decided I had to join, too. As soon as I got home, I applied."

It wasn't long before Cunard realized that Ron Warwick, like his father, was made of the right maritime stuff. The younger man quickly rose through the

From left to right:
Captain Arthur Rostron and
Captain James Bissett;
Commodore William Warwick;
Queen Elizabeth maiden voyage;
Commodore William Warwick.

©Harvey Lloyd

Captain Ronald W. Warwick

ranks. By 1990, in fact, he was commanding *QE2*, the first time a Cunard master had captained the same ship as his father.

Five years later, retired Commodore Warwick returned to the liner as a passenger on *QE2*'s first round-Britain cruise. As the vessel sailed into Liverpool, both Warwicks stood proudly on the bridge.

Now Ron Warwick is taking his place on the bridge of *QM2*. "I am just thrilled to be a part of it," he says. "It is an immense honour to take command of such a grand ship, and I am keen to ensure that *QM2* lives up to the best Cunard traditions."

Warwick says his only regret is that his father is not here to see him take the helm. William Warwick passed away in 1998, before Cunard had even begun to plan *QM2*. But the commodore's seafaring spirit lives on in his son.

"He would have been proud," Warwick says, "very proud."

Turning
dreams
into reality

No ship has ever been

designed like QM2

- a liner which sets the benchmark

for others, extends the boundaries

of ship design and which

is far ahead of any passenger ship

in the fields of comfort, safety

and environmental protection.

The QM2 project represents

for ALSTOM Marine - the designer and

builder of the legendary Normandie

and France liners - the consecration

of its know-how and confirms

its position among the leaders

in the construction of

high added-value ships.

ALSTOM | Marine

www.marine.alstom.com

We run a tight ship.

We wish
Queen Mary 2
fair winds and
happy voyages

ABB is a leading manufacturer and system supplier of safe and reliable power plants and electric propulsion systems. Today, most cruise ships in operation or under construction worldwide are designed to ABB's propulsion concept. ABB has more than 60 years of experience in engineering and supplying electrical and automation systems for merchant, naval and offshore vessels. ABB provides total system responsibility, including engineering, manufacturing, supplying, installation, startup and service.

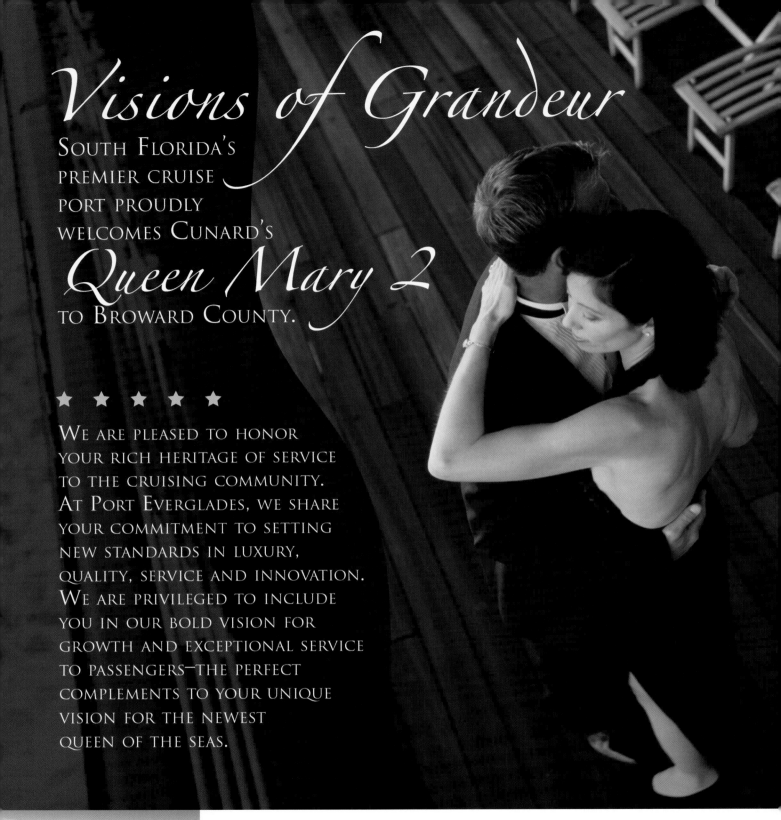

Visions of Grandeur

SOUTH FLORIDA'S
PREMIER CRUISE
PORT PROUDLY
WELCOMES CUNARD'S

Queen Mary 2

TO BROWARD COUNTY.

★ ★ ★ ★ ★

WE ARE PLEASED TO HONOR
YOUR RICH HERITAGE OF SERVICE
TO THE CRUISING COMMUNITY.
AT PORT EVERGLADES, WE SHARE
YOUR COMMITMENT TO SETTING
NEW STANDARDS IN LUXURY,
QUALITY, SERVICE AND INNOVATION.
WE ARE PRIVILEGED TO INCLUDE
YOU IN OUR BOLD VISION FOR
GROWTH AND EXCEPTIONAL SERVICE
TO PASSENGERS—THE PERFECT
COMPLEMENTS TO YOUR UNIQUE
VISION FOR THE NEWEST
QUEEN OF THE SEAS.

PORT EVERGLADES
BROWARD COUNTY, FLORIDA

1850 Eller Drive • Ft. Lauderdale, FL 33316 • 954.523.3404 • www.broward.org/port

Paul | Weiss

congratulates

Carnival Corporation
and
Cunard Line

on the inauguration of the

Queen Mary 2

1285 Avenue of the Americas
New York, NY 10019-6094
phone 212.373.3000
fax 212.757.3990
email mailbox@paulweiss.com

NEW YORK ◆ WASHINGTON, DC ◆ LONDON ◆ PARIS ◆ TOKYO ◆ BEIJING ◆ HONG KONG

PAUL, WEISS, RIFKIND, WHARTON & GARRISON LLP

www.paulweiss.com

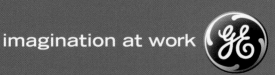

the dream

©Harvey Lloyd

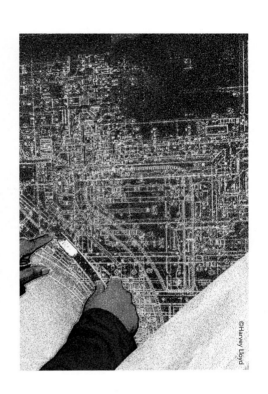

©Harvey Lloyd

"And see! she stirs!

She starts – she moves –
she seems to feel

The thrill of life along
her keel."

–Henry Wadsworth

birth of a legend

©Harvey Lloyd

Queen Mary 2, the world's greatest ocean liner, began as the dream of a little boy.

By his own admission, Cunard newbuilds director, Gerry Ellis, has the greatest job in the world. "It's fantastic," says the man who has helped to make the new *Queen Mary 2* – the first true ocean liner in three decades – a reality. "One minute I'll be talking to the shipyard about refrigeration units and the next I'll be meeting with the art consultants, looking at paintings."

Ellis is perched at his desk in Cunard's Miami headquarters, trying to make a dent in his e-mail, but two new messages seem to come in for each one answered. Around him, the office straddles a line between workmanlike organisation and creative clutter. On every flat surface are stacks of blueprints, equipment catalogs, signage proofs, and artists' renderings, all mortared together with samples of decking materials and fabrics. On the shelves, volumes of technical specs stand alongside books detailing the history of the 20th-century ocean liner, including numerous volumes on Cunard history. On the wall, two large, framed, black-and-white photos depict the original *Queen Mary* at the beginning and end of her career, entering New York harbor on her 1936 maiden voyage and arriving in Long Beach 31 years later, ready to be converted into a hotel and tourist attraction.

Staffers march in and out of his office, filling the large inbox on one side of Ellis' desk, occasionally stopping to raid a drawer of sweets behind his chair. Like the deck officer he was for most of his career, Ellis is calm amid the hubbub, happy to sit back and explain the process of building the largest, costliest, most advanced passenger vessel of all time. Dipping to root around in a thick file box on the floor, he plucks out a single page, slightly dog-eared and seemingly nondescript, with "Capital Expenditure

From left to right:
Stephen Payne, Captain Ronald Warwick, and Gerry Ellis; Artist rendering of aft promenade; Stephen Payne.

Request" across the top. It's a standard document any company might use to process the costs of doing business – only this one is a bit different. "This," he says with the slightest grin, "is where I asked for $800 million to build an ocean liner."

Dreaming the Dream Ship

QM2 didn't begin there, though. It began in the mind of a precocious little boy.

Stephen M. Payne was born in London in 1960 to a family that had never left the UK's shores, but a sort of seafaring wanderlust hit him in 1968, after he watched a BBC news program on the classic Cunarder, *Queen Elizabeth*. Later, on a visit to Southampton Docks, Payne and his father toured the newly commissioned *Queen Elizabeth 2* and watched the legendary liner *United States* enter port on one of her final pre-layup voyages. The boy was hooked.

After he read an article claiming there would never be another legendary ocean liner, he wrote to Cunard "to say there might be, and even suggested some ideas for its design." A few years later, during a Southampton-to-Cherbourg sailing aboard *QE2*, he made the decision to devote his career to naval architecture.

After graduating from Southampton University with honours in 1984, Payne went to work for Carnival Corporate Technical Services (now Carnival Corporate Shipbuilding) in London. Early on he was involved in building the Fun Ship *Holiday*. Design work on Carnival's *Fantasy-* and *Destiny*-class vessels followed, as did work on Holland America Line's *Statendam* class and new flagship, *Rotterdam VI*. He is now Carnival Corporation's senior naval architect and project manager, designing and writing specs for the company's newbuilds, supervising plan approval, and dispatching teams to the shipyards to oversee construction.

In April 1998, Carnival Corporation purchased Cunard from Norway's Kvaerner Group, which had acquired the line only two years before through its takeover of Britain's Trafalgar House. Calling Cunard "the strongest brand name in the luxury segment of the cruise market" and citing *QE2*'s reputation as the best-known passenger ship in the world, Carnival chairman and CEO Micky Arison set about returning the company to what it does best: operating ocean liners. The line's smaller ships were quickly transferred to other brands in the Carnival empire, leaving Cunard free to concentrate on its two true liners, *QE2* and the former Norwegian American vessel, *Vistafjord*, which has since been renamed *Caronia*.

But the big news was still to come. "Buying the company only made sense if we were going to grow it," says Arison, "and in keeping with Cunard's heritage, that meant a liner." So on June 8, 1998, barely two months after the acquisition, Cunard announced that the line would begin "Project *Queen Mary*," to develop the first true ocean liner since *QE2*. "It is our objective," he said, "to build a new generation of ocean liner that will be the

From left to right: *QM2* sea trials; *QM2* at the shipyard; Micky Arison.

very pinnacle of the shipbuilder's art, the realisation of a dream of another time. Our goal is nothing less than to create a new Golden Age of sea travel for those who missed the first."

An Ocean Liner in a Cruise Ship World

Ronald Warwick, the *QE2* captain who would go on to take the helm of the new *QM2*, was elated. "I felt Carnival Corporation had delivered a message to the world that they were determined to build on the legacy Sir Samuel Cunard had left for us."

Appropriately, Stephen Payne had first heard news of Project *Queen Mary* while sailing across the Atlantic on *QE2*. "The big question was, would the new ship be for transatlantic service? I felt it had to be a real liner."

But what exactly is a liner? Such vessels are designed to sail between two points, maintaining a strict schedule despite adverse weather conditions. The North Atlantic, on which Cunard's ships have sailed for 164 years, is full of icebergs in spring, crisscrossed by Atlantic hurricanes in summer and fall, and wracked by waves and bitter winds in winter. Unlike a cruise ship, a Cunard liner has ports that can be skipped to regain time lost to bad weather, so she must have sufficient reserve, toughness, and hydrodynamic efficiency to soldier on, even in conditions that would force a typical cruise ship to cut her speed by half.

Thus, *QM2* would be a departure from the way most modern ships are built. Typically, the choreography is standard: Cruise line decides to build new ship. Line talks to shipyards explaining what it wants. Line comes to agreement with one yard to design and build the vessel. Champagne corks pop.

Though *QM2* would be a radical departure from other ships in today's market, Carnival Corporation and Cunard Line assumed initially that her trajectory would follow some version of this route, and so solicited a speculative design from a noted yard in Europe. The result, delivered early in summer 1998, was not quite what they had in mind. Instead of a sleek North Atlantic greyhound, the vessel was, as Payne remembers it, "a cruise ship that looked like an ocean liner." While the vessel would be perfect for sailing around the Caribbean or Mediterranean, and acceptable for the occasional transatlantic repositioning, it was wrong for the kind of hard use to which Cunard intended to put its new ship. Arison told Payne to come up with his own design, but Payne had only two weeks to present a first plan.

Working with junior assistant architect Rick Moore, Payne quickly completed a general layout that reflected his vision for the new vessel, which he presented to Micky Arison; Carnival vice chairman, CFO Howard Frank; and Cunard COO Pamela Conover. The group gave their approval almost immediately, along with a few words of wisdom. "Micky said, 'I suspect you'll only get one chance in your life to design a ship like this, so you'd better get it right the first time.' "

from dream to drafting board

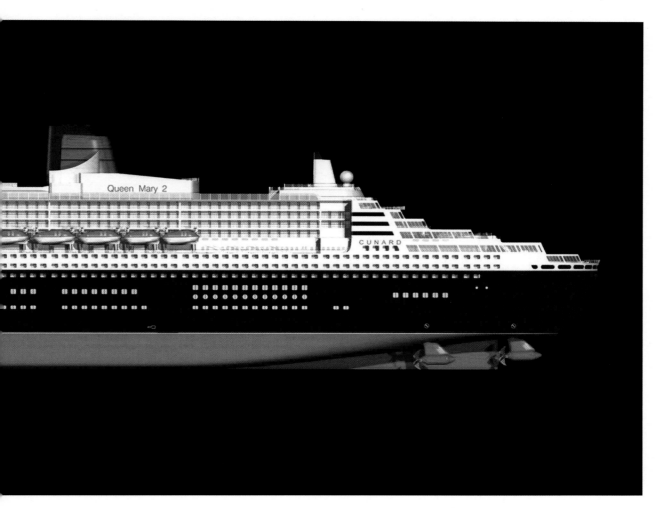

designing *QM2* was a major undertaking,
but the results have been well worth the effort.

"Everyone has an idea of how a passenger ship should look. She should be long and sleek, her dark hull fronted by a knife-sharp bow."

In late summer of 1998, Cunard Line began to assemble the team that would take *Queen Mary 2* from vision to reality. At the helm was Stephen Payne, Carnival Corporation's senior naval architect; at his side, Gerry Ellis, Cunard's first newbuilds director in a quarter of a century.

Payne and Ellis both had extensive knowledge of liner history and construction. A native of the Wirral, Merseyside, UK, Ellis was 16 when he went to sea aboard a cargo ship. After graduating from Liverpool University, he logged 25 seafaring years as a cargo ship commander and, later, as first officer on *QE2*. In addition, he brought to Project *Queen Mary* three years as itinerary planner and port operations manager at Cunard's Miami headquarters.

"My experience as a deck officer complemented what Stephen brought to the project," Ellis says. "Stephen knows ocean liners, but day-to-day operations aren't part of a naval architect's discipline. You need someone who can tell you where the ship will need extra protection from the weather, where she'll need drain holes in the bulkheads, how the bridge layout needs to be designed, and so on."

In a sense, Payne's and Ellis' challenge was the polar opposite of what naval architects faced in the 1960s, when the rise of air travel over shipping meant designers reared on the cold North Atlantic had to begin designing for the sunny Caribbean as well. Some adapted, some did not. Conversely, when the Cunard team went to work, they were attempting to design an ocean liner for an industry that had made only cruise ships for the past three decades. The canvas upon which *Queen Mary 2* would be drawn was blank. But if there was pressure, there also was exhilaration. "It was a dream come true for me," says

Payne. "It was something I'd had ideas for since the age of 12."

Everyone has an idea of how a passenger ship should look. She should be long and sleek, her dark hull fronted by a knife-sharp bow. Her bridge should be set back foursquare on the very top deck, its wings stretching port to starboard like a 19th-century gentleman's mustache. Surmounting all, her stacks – preferably three or four – should rise tall and angled for speed, giving a reassuring impression of power. Look deep enough, and you'd probably find that most people still envision a ship's top decks festooned with those curious curved air funnels from which film comedians were always emerging in the 1930s and 1940s, although hardly anyone would remember what they were for or that they haven't been needed since the advent of air conditioning.

That these stereotypical images have persisted to the present day is one of the most remarkable testaments to the ocean liner's mystique, since not one of those elements has survived in the modern cruise ship. But the romantic aesthetic to which the public clings is based on scientific principles. More than a matter of looks, the shape of a ship's hull determines its essential character.

You begin with a basic, rectangular box. Leaving it in this original shape would obviously yield the largest amount of interior space for passengers and cargo, but such a shape would limit its hydrodynamic efficiency, precluding any significant speed through the water. The design of oil tankers is the best example of this. The typical cruise ship is an improvement, but the same need to maximize interior space mandates that it retain a certain rectangularity, its hull flaring to full width only a short distance

From left to right:
Artist rendering of discotheque; Artist rendering of the health club; Bow of QM2 under construction.

back from the bow, its superstructure rising high and straight for almost its entire length. Conversely, to achieve the 30-knot speed she'd need for her transatlantic service, *Queen Mary 2* would need to be long and lean, able to slice cleanly through the water like her older sister *QE2*.

Harsh sea conditions also mandated that *QM2*'s superstructure would differ significantly from the cruise ship norm. Forward, she would need to be tapered and set far back, with anchor winches and other mooring equipment installed below decks rather than on the long, open forecastle, to minimize the possibility of damage from large rogue waves. *QM2*'s bridge face would be similar to *QE2*'s and to the Golden Age liners: of heavy steel, set with small, thick windows rather than the floor-to-ceiling walls of glass common on cruise ships. And whereas a cruiser's bridge tends to be set comparatively low on the superstructure, leaving room for observation lounges on the decks above, *QM2*'s bridge would be in the traditional top-deck position.

Potential heavy seas also ruled out cabins and public rooms being positioned high on the stern, as is the norm on cruise ships. On the North Atlantic, these

©Harvey Lloyd

©Harvey Lloyd

rooms potentially would be subject to an uncomfortable amount of pitching and rolling, so for *QM2*, the kind of stepped fantail superstructure seen on *QE2* and most other classic liners would be employed. Below this, in the hull, a traditional rounded cruiser stern was mandated, but at the waterline it would be married to a flat bottom, the combination providing the optimal performance. In calm seas, the smooth bottom would aid in speed, providing a flat wake, but in heavy weather the rounded stern would dip into the water as the vessel pitched, thus aiding stability.

The difficulty, from a business perspective, was that the cruise ship model was developed for a reason: profitability. The taller and more straight-sided the ship, the more revenue-producing cabins she can accommodate. To be fast, however, and thus fulfill her mandate as a liner, *QM2* would require a

liner's shape, and that would mean that more than one-fifth of her tonnage – from the tip of her bow back to the bridge, and on the top three or four decks in the stern – would be lost to revenue. Not an easy proposal to make in today's economy. Adding to the problem was the fact that to ensure her strength and long life, the ship's hull steel would have to be uncommonly thick, measuring between 0.9 and 1.1 inches (23 and 28 millimeters), compared with about 0.7 inches (18 millimeters) average on similar-size cruise vessels. This naturally increases the vessel's weight, which increases her power demands and, thus, her operating costs. The high speeds necessary for the transatlantic trade make this problem more acute, since speed and propulsive power are not proportional; increasing power by, say, 35 percent, gains you only an additional 11 percent in speed. For this reason, *Queen Mary 2*

From left to right:
Deck under construction at dusk;
Staircase of atrium interior; Artist
rendering of the penthouse balcony.

would be built to generate a remarkable 86 megawatts of propulsive power, compared with the 42 megawatts that drive Royal Caribbean International's 138,000-ton *Voyager*-class ships.

But Carnival and Cunard took the long view on issues of operability and profits. "Once I demonstrated why a true liner was needed for the Atlantic, I had no problems from the company regarding the ship type," says Payne. Still, *QM2* could not be art for art's sake. "Everything I did had to balance the real needs of a transatlantic ship with its earning potential, providing enough revenue through the number of cabins, bars, and the like to justify its enormous expense."

Some traditional ocean liner elements did not survive the costing-out process. For example, a plan to allow *QM2* to transport cars was nixed early on because of fire regulations and lack of space.

Similarly, the concept of a traditional indoor promenade, glassed in and completely encircling one deck, was disposed of early. In its place, the Cunard team developed an innovative alternative: a wide passage that's part corridor and part observation lounge, snaking from Decks 2 to 3 via stairways and sometimes running between the decks, courtesy of the Britannia restaurant's taller-at-the-center-than-the-sides shape.

Tradition and practicality merged as well in the design of *QM2*'s single funnel. While nostalgia suggested a three-stack design after the manner of the original *Queen Mary*, logic did not. "They simply weren't needed," says Payne, noting that the redundant stacks would have been cosmetic only. "Cunard had never had a vessel built with dummy funnels, and my feeling was that anything false would detract from the ship."

There also were several technical reasons for having just one funnel, including stability, reduced windage, and better smoke dispersal – not to mention maintaining the family resemblance between *QM2* and her illustrious older sibling, *QE2*.

Getting There Is Half the Fun

When *QE2* set sail in 1969, the growing popularity of air travel already had crippled many of Cunard's competitors. Thus, *QE2* represented a gamble for the line. But the ship clearly was a different kind of ocean liner, at that point the most successful ever at merging the needs of a liner and those of a cruise ship. It was, therefore, natural that in designing *QM2* for warm-climate cruising as well as Atlantic crossing, Payne would look to the older

ship as a model. But lessons learned from the modern cruise industry also proved valuable.

To meet the demands of luxury-minded passengers, eight cabin decks were designed with balconies, representing an astounding 94 percent of *QM2*'s outside accommodations, and great care was taken to protect them from North Atlantic weather. Lower balconies (on Decks 4, 5, and 6, below Boat Deck) are recessed into the steel of the hull to provide protection, with their cabins set back nearly 10 feet from the rail. In the superstructure, sheer height above the waterline provides protection.

In her stern, *QM2*'s deep, tiered decks would be designed to reflect the nominal class structure adapted from *QE2*, with the wide aftward swath of Deck 11 reserved for Queens Grill passengers, the Pool Terrace on Deck 8 for use by adults,

Naval Architecture 101

The basic equation by which naval architects determine the shape of their hulls – and thus their speed – is called the block coefficient: $Cb = V / (L \times B \times T)$. In this equation, V represents the total underwater volume of the ship, L and B represent its length and breadth at the waterline, and T represents its draft, or the depth to which the hull falls below the water.

A rectangle has a block coefficient of 1. The more you shave off that 1, the faster your ship will be. The typical tanker has a block coefficient hovering around .90, most cruise ships measure just above .70, and a fast warship like a destroyer measures around .40. *Queen Mary 2*'s block coefficient is a low .61, just slightly above *QE2*'s very low .58.

and the Minnows Pool area two decks below dedicated to children. Up on Deck 13, *QM2*'s main pool would have a retractable roof to enable its use in all climates, and would be air-conditioned and heated as necessary.

For walkers, the outdoor promenade would circle the entire ship in the traditional fashion, lined with steamer chairs and wide enough for passengers to walk four abreast, but there would be a difference: In harsh weather, walkers would round the bow behind a solid steel wall, while in better conditions a pair of large doors would remain open to allow a full outdoor circuit. It's a concept Payne borrowed from one of his favorite liners, Holland America Line's *Rotterdam V*, which also influenced the design of Deck 13's outdoor observation area.

If *QE2* acted as a general model for a multiple-use ocean liner, for Gerry Ellis she also acted quite literally as a guide to the world's ports. "When I came into the project I started looking almost immediately into the port situation, using *QE2* as a measuring stick. I knew that if *QE2* were too long or deep to enter a port, then *QM2* would not be able to enter there either. However, where the issue is sheer manoeuverability, *QM2*'s greater facility in this regard might allow her to get in where *QE2* has trouble."

The new vessel's height was one of the most important factors, as it would determine her ability to pass under bridges and the kinds of electrical and telecommunications cables that frequently stretch across a harbour's entrance. On the American side of her

Artist renderings from left to right: The pool; the Winter Garden.

transatlantic run, the bar of entrance to New York Harbor is set by the Verrazano Narrows Bridge, which provides 216 feet of clearance from the waterline. The Cunard team took into account the worst possible conditions – the highest tide, the hottest weather (which causes the bridge to sag), and the lightest the ship could possibly sail – and set QM2's final air draught at 203 feet, providing 13 feet of breathing room.

Along with concerns about QM2's ability to navigate into the ports was the question of her ability to dock there, since her length would require extremely long piers and her weight and windage would exert tremendous pull on the docking bollards. "I began e-mailing QE2's ports – about 150 in total – sending them the new ship's statistics to determine if they could accommodate her," Ellis says. "Less than 10 percent said their piers weren't up to the task, so at

those ports we'll have to bring people ashore by tender."

Another of Ellis' duties at this stage was to look at Payne's plans from the perspective of regulations and deck operations. "What Stephen produced in August 1998 was very similar to the final design, but with a different engine arrangement, different bridge arrangement, and different arrangement of decks. The mooring decks, for instance, were originally too high, and also had to be lengthened to make her easier to tie up at New York's short finger piers. Because of her length, she'll overhang the end of her dock there, and we needed to run ropes aft from the stern, rather than forward."

One of the most important regulatory issues concerned Rule 24 of the International Convention for the Safety of Life at Sea (SOLAS), which mandates that the height of lifeboat davits may not

Setting New Standards

London's venerable Lloyd's Register, which has been judging the safety of passenger and cargo vessels since the 1760s, acted as QM2's "classification society" from the beginning, ensuring that every part of her was designed and built to the most exacting specifications.

Because the standard by which cruise ships are built was not sufficiently stringent for a true ocean liner, a new standard had to be developed by which everything critical to the ship's safety would be judged, from upholstery materials to fire plans, engine machinery, steel thickness, and the types of welds used.

Supporting steelwork needed to be particularly strong, so main bulkheads were stiffened in a fore-and-aft position rather than horizontally, and the steel web framing – the structural supports that ring the ship's girth and run along her length – was designed to be about 30 percent denser than aboard a traditional cruise ship.

Artist renderings from left to right:
The Atrium; The Queens room;
The Britannia restaurant.

exceed 49.2 feet (15 meters) from the waterline – a logical distance in normal seas, but too low for the North Atlantic. Knowing that the regulations allow for exemptions on the basis of practicality, ship size, and the weather conditions likely to be encountered, Ellis and Payne brought QE2's operational records to the UK's Marine Coast Guard Agency and the U.S. Coast Guard, showing that even at a height of 88.5 feet (27 meters) – the same distance being proposed for QM2 – her lifeboats had occasionally sustained wave damage on the Atlantic. In the face of this evidence, an exemption was granted almost immediately.

As esoteric and tangential as the issue of lifeboat placement might sound, it was in fact a central question, since the height of the boats affected not only QM2's exterior profile but also the arrangement of her decks; as it is Cunard's practice to muster passengers indoors and not on the open deck, the boats had to be mounted on a deck with sufficient public space inside, rather than cabins. With this hurdle overcome, the Cunard team was free to finalize the interior layout of the ship.

The Cunard Look

Different cruise lines have different ways of handling their interiors. Some design by committee, with a dozen or more professionals pooling their efforts, while others assign their interiors to a

single expert. For *QM2*, Cunard wanted the best of both worlds.

Founded by interior designer Robert Tillberg, Tillberg/SMC has specialized in creating the interiors of passenger vessels for some 40 years, beginning with Swedish-American Line's *Kungsholm* in 1966 and continuing through vessels like Crystal Cruises' *Crystal Symphony* in 1995 and Disney Cruise Line's *Disney Wonder* in 1998 – to date, some 110 cruise ships, ferries, and luxury yachts in all. The company's association with Cunard began with its 1990 refit of *QE2*, followed by similar jobs on *Sagafjord* and *Vistfjord* in 1993/94. "They made a nice job of it," says Ellis. "We liked the look. It was very traditional. It was us – the Cunard look. So, when it came time to design the interior of *QM2*, we naturally turned to them as well."

The Tillberg team – beginning with Fredrik Johansson and his colleagues

in Viken, Sweden, and later expanding to include designers Chris Finch and Anna Bengtsson, graphic designer Keith Allen, and materials specialists Anita Bell and Anna Soderlindh, all working under project manager Andrew Collier – was part of Project *Queen Mary* from day one, attending early meetings with Payne, Ellis, and COO Pamela Conover. From the start, all the participants knew they wanted continuity with the past – "the opulence, elegance, and class of a traditional Cunard vessel, built for today's modern world," as Conover describes it – but they also wanted to buck some more recent trends.

"The whole idea was that it was designed to get away from the modern idea of an inward-looking ship," says Ellis. "Whereas with some cruise ships today you can be aboard and hardly know you're on the ocean, with *QM2*

we wanted the sea to always be a backdrop."

Since *QM2* was being designed from the outside in – that is, tailored to the demands of the North Atlantic – the Tillberg team had to fit its designs into Payne's vision. This was, however, less a problem than a blessing. For instance, Payne's ingenious arrangement of the public decks, two of them low in the hull (where no balconies could be fitted) and the third on Deck 7, with the lifeboats hanging between Decks 7 and 8, made it possible to design nearly 80 percent of passenger accommodations with sea views.

The size and high passenger-space ratio of *QM2* would also allow a greater diversity of public areas than had ever been possible with ocean liners or most cruise ships. Grandeur was guaranteed, with spaces like the Queens Room ballroom and the Royal Court Theatre designed to be among the largest and

Artist renderings from left to right:
The Veuve Clicquot Champagne Bar;
The Kings Court.

most luxurious at sea, but there would also be intimate spaces, such as the Commodore Club observation lounge/jazz club and the traditionally designed Golden Lion pub.

Accommodation would similarly run the gamut, from stately suites to inside cabins that, at 194 square feet, are some 20 percent larger than the industry average. At the upper end, the Queen Mary and Queen Elizabeth suites in the bow would extend out below the bridge wings for 180-degree views forward, back, and to the sides, and each would offer key-only access via private glass elevators. In the stern, five duplex apartments would be the most lavish afloat, with upstairs bedroom areas set back like an indoor balcony, providing full-height views aft through two-deck glass windows.

Some elements of the design process were evolutionary, such as development of the 500-seat Illuminations auditorium, part of the Cunard ConneXions learning center complex. "I was looking at a cross-section plan one day," says Ellis, "and we had a lecture hall with a cinema screen and a stage, and I thought, 'Well, what if we had the screen continue up over the audience's heads? Then we could project IMAX films and the like.' I made a sketch

to see if it was feasible, then thought, 'If we can do that, what about a planetarium?' "

After a trip to the London Planetarium to see the Digistar II projection system in action, Ellis returned to Miami fired up by the concept, eventually hiring the London firm designteam to bring it to life. "They were able to immediately grasp what we were looking for, and had always worked with lighting and graphic designers," says Ellis. "The Tillberg look is very traditional and classy, but we felt that this area, as well as the Todd English specialty restaurant, required a different approach – classy as well, with an Art Deco feel, but approached in a more modern way. Since the firm was already acknowledged as the best in designing onboard shopping, we gave them the contract for Deck 3's Mayfair Shops area as well."

Though QM2 would be designed with the most modern methods and materials available, it was also inevitable that Cunard's long, rich history would lead to more traditional approaches. "When we began the project," says Tillberg's Johansson, "we did extensive research on historic liners, naturally concentrating on Cunard ships like Queen Mary, but also on some of the French liners like Ile-De-France, L'Atlantique, and Normandie. What these ships all had in common was a beautiful clarity and symmetry in their layouts as well as a rather formal elegance."

Outright mimicry of *Queen Mary* or the other Golden Age liners was, however, out of the question, both for philosophic and regulatory reasons. "We wanted to revive some of what made the Golden Age ships so stunning," says Johansson, "but without making just a pastiche of the past." Any nostalgic desire to honour *Queen Mary*'s reputation as "the ship of beautiful woods" would simply not be possible because of international safety rules due to take effect in 2010, which mandate that no flammable materials be used in wall paneling, stair banisters, or any other aspect of a passenger vessel's interior structure. Even furniture and smaller fixtures, such as picture frames, will be limited, based on the fire-load calculation for each individual room. This put the kibosh on some wonderful opportunities that presented themselves early on, as when a family-owned

company that had created ornate wooden paneling for the original *Queen Mary* contacted Ellis, offering its services for *QM2*.

Though outright duplication of yesteryear was a non-issue, homage and influence certainly have their place in *QM2*'s interiors. The Tillberg team's design for the 1,351-seat Britannia Restaurant, for instance, recalls *Queen Mary*'s magnificent 800-seat first-class restaurant, with a vaulted, back-lit glass ceiling inspired by the stained-glass skylights of early 20th-century French liners. Similarly, Deck 7's Winter Garden, an airy, greenery-filled lounge space for afternoon tea, was designed after the skylighted verandah cafés and palm courts of vessels like Cunard's *Mauretania*. On Deck 8 aft, *QM2*'s Todd English alternative restaurant hearkens back to *Queen Mary*'s similarly situated Verandah Grill, one of that vessel's most legendary spaces.

History at Every Turn

Cunard history is on display along *QM2*'s Maritime Quest heritage trail. Designed by London's Open Agency, the *QE2*-inspired route winds throughout the ship, with a timeline of Cunard history displayed on huge boards in the stairtower landings and in portions of the interior promenade. Further information is available via touch-screen displays, and portable audio wands provide commentary at each station.

building a queen

©Harvey Lloyd

from nuts and bolts to bells and whistles, constructing a liner of the new *Queen Mary 2*' s stature is no small undertaking.

In summer 1999, planning for *QM2* had reached the point where Cunard was ready to negotiate for her construction. Under consideration were five competing shipyards: Fincantieri of Monfalcone, Italy; Kvaerner Masa-Yards of Turku, Finland; Howaldtswerke-Deutsche Werft AG of Kiel, Germany; Alstom's Chantiers de l'Atlantique of St-Nazaire, France; and Harland & Wolff of Belfast, Northern Ireland.

Each yard received the latest version of the general arrangement plan, a mini-spec describing the ship's intended service and capabilities, a makers' list naming acceptable manufacturers of major machinery and systems, and a directive that per-square-meter bids were to be based on Holland America Line's *Rotterdam VI.* As added assurance that the yards would understand what Cunard expected, senior architect Stephen Payne took the unprecedented step of specifying a 40-year fatigue life for the vessel.

"Knowing how expensive she'd be," he recalls, "I thought she should have a long life. I also thought this would force the shipyards to provide a ship of substantial quality, built to last." It was probably the first time such a requirement was ever made at the inception of a passenger ship's construction.

The field narrowed quickly and in short order the decision was down to two yards: Harland & Wolff and Chantiers. Both had illustrious histories. Chantiers, established in 1861, had been responsible for such legendary liners as *Ile de France, Normandie,* and *France* as well as more modern cruise vessels like Radisson Seven Seas Cruises' *Paul Gauguin* and Celebrity Cruises' *Millennium.*

Harland & Wolff, established in 1853, had produced the great White Star liners *Oceanic, Olympic,* and the legendary *Titanic*, but in recent decades had concentrated on construction of oil tankers and drillships. Harland & Wolff's experience with building strong ships for arduous conditions made the yard well-suited for Project *Queen Mary*. But a cruise newbuild was another matter. Initially, Harland & Wolff had partnered with *Germany*'s Lloyd Werft yard for the vessel's outfitting, but then that company pulled out of the deal.

The job went to Chantiers. "Chantiers' track record and recent vast improvements in their industrial processes gave them the edge," says Cunard newbuilds director Gerry Ellis. On March 9, 2000, Cunard and Chantiers announced they had signed a letter of intent, and the construction phase of Project *Queen Mary* was on.

A Queen Emerges

Although finalizing plans for *QM2*'s construction was proving a long, difficult process, expectations of her launch were building steadily. By November 2000, when the new ship was just a series of drawings, specifications, and computer models, some 600 prospective cruisers already had sent Cunard checks to secure passage on *QM2*'s maiden voyage. It would be another 18 months before the date of that voyage was even announced. Anticipation was growing – and so was *QM2*.

Until the shipyard selection phase, plans had called for the vessel to measure 110,000 tons and 1,115 feet long, with capacity for approximately 1,900. But by the time Cunard selected Chantiers, the company announced that the new ship would weigh in at 150,000 gross tons,

stretch to 1,132 feet, and accommodate 2,620 passengers.

Profitability was a factor in this decision. The per-bed cost at 110,000 tonnes was too high. Stability tests also indicated that the ship would benefit from a wider beam. Payne's team adopted a "tumble home" design that stretched her hull wider at the waterline than at the boat deck, increasing her volume in the water without increasing her draught. This set in motion a chain of alterations.

To maintain her hydrodynamic ratio and thus her speed, the ship's hull would need to be lengthened, though not drastically. The total increase in size also meant *QM2* would require changes in her power and propulsion, so her design was altered from a central propeller and two Mermaid Pods (self-contained propulsion units mounted beneath the hull) to four pods, two of them fixed and two able to swivel 360 degrees, providing extreme manoeuverability. On the suggestion of Chantiers, two of her diesel engines were also replaced by funnel-mounted gas turbines, a system the shipyard was using in the construction of Princess Cruises' *Coral Princess*. This freed up interior space that had been occupied by the diesels and their emissions uptakes,

which in turn allowed the Cunard team to alter the layout of *QM2*'s public decks, creating the wide central corridors we see today on Decks 2 and 3. This allows passengers an even greater sense of the sea as they enter rooms like Sir Samuel's wine bar, the Golden Lion pub, and the Chart Room lounge.

What followed was an intense eight-month period of negotiation, in which Cunard and Chantiers fine-tuned *QM2*'s design and butted heads over her needs. Once again, it was the peculiar demands of the North Atlantic that created the greatest difficulties. For instance, even though *QM2*'s bow is some two decks higher than *QE2*'s, Cunard knew the forward-facing windows on the superstructure would need additional protection from waves, and so mandated steel shutters that could be affixed in heavy weather.

"This was totally alien to the shipyard," says Gerry Ellis. "They'd never heard of anything like it. They said, 'You don't need anything like that. It's only water, and the glass is reinforced.' But we said, 'No, no, we're talking about *the whole front end of the ship going underwater.'*" Photos of storm damage suffered by *QE2* over the years ultimately proved their case.

On November 6, 2000, having come to agreement on *Queen Mary 2*'s general arrangement and specifications; technical and outfitting standards to which she'd be built; a December 2003, delivery date; and a price of $780 million, Cunard and Chantiers signed the final contract for *QM2*'s construction.

From this point, the ship's overall plan remained largely unchanged, though innumerable meetings were required to ensure that the line and yard were on the

same page on design, equipment, and construction, beginning with the engine layout and proceeding in stages all the way through outfitting. From London, the Carnival Corporate Shipbuilding team – including senior naval architect Jeff Frier, senior marine engineer Matt Suatt, electrical engineers David Storer and Mike Crawley, and safety engineer Tom Strang, along with personnel in charge of electrics, plumbing, air conditioning, information systems, paints and coatings, and other technical matters – worked with their French counterparts to flesh out the general arrangement into the full, final specification.

Meanwhile, Payne, Ellis, and their team took *QM2*'s design on the road to test its efficacy in simulated conditions. In February 2001, the group traveled to Maritime Research International (MARIN) in Wageningen, the Netherlands, where a scale model of *QM2* – constructed from

hull-form drawings and fitted with precise miniatures of the pods, stabilizers, and propellers – was put through a battery of tests in the facility's huge model basins. Free to move on its own, the 15-foot model and its monitoring sensors were connected by an umbilical cord to a platform above, from which technicians recorded data on pitch, roll, hull pressure, speed, and manoeuverability under varying conditions. The model performed exactly as predicted, breasting a simulated 40-foot swell at 18 knots, with almost no water coming over the bow.

The next stop was Lyngby, Denmark, for smoke and comfort tests at the facilities of the Danish Maritime Institute. There, scale models of the various exhaust tubes in *QM2*'s funnel mimicked the exact exhaust pressure they'd experience in actual use. Because different gasses leave the tubes at different scales and speeds, the mix had

to be adjusted so that all the gasses would blow out together, passing far above passengers on *QM2*'s stern decks. In another test, the bright blue ship model was strewn with yellow cracked wheat and then run through varying wind conditions as cameras rolled. Caught on film, whorls and other movement patterns in the wheat indicated where extra wind breaks would be required on the ship's decks.

During this time, the French yard continued to hone aspects of the final design as well, often creating mockups of machinery to ensure that everything would work as it was supposed to and meet Cunard's high standards. Equipment and materials ordered from outside suppliers also were subjected to rigorous testing, first at the factory before delivery and then at the shipyard.

Among the equipment were some 34,000 tonnes of steel, ready to be shaped into *Queen Mary 2*'s sleek hull. On January 16, 2002, Cunard President Pamela Conover, surrounded by representatives of the line, the shipyard, and the international media, activated a machine that cut the very first steel sheet of hull number G32, a.k.a. *Queen Mary 2*. The dream was finally becoming reality.

The Course Is Set

In the old days, ships were built entirely on a central building berth, with all of their elements – plates, framework, pipes, ventilation ducts, and other machinery – brought in from the surrounding shipyard and secured in place within the vessel's growing skeleton. Today, the process is decentralized, with different sections of the vessel constructed in different parts of the yard, giving more working space than would be possible in the confines of the ship itself.

In constructing *QM2*, Chantiers employed some 3,600 workers on site, overseen by project managers Alain Crouzols and Jean-Remy Villagois and construction manager Etienne Lamock. An inspection team representing Carnival Corporation and Cunard, led by project manager Soren Krogsgaard and deputy Eric Lewis, coordinated the architects and ensured that the ship was being built and outfitted to specifications. Several hundred men and women were employed in different specialised prefabrications shops responsible for cutting and forming raw steel sheets into *QM2*'s decks and bulkheads. In a separate workshop, shaping specialists created all the curved pieces of the vessel – hull plating, bow bulb, and superstructure – using a roller capable of applying 3,000 tons of pressure. From here, these elements were subject to the first stages of prefitting before being sent on to the yard's vast preassembly area,

which was 0.6 mile long and 164 feet wide (one kilometer long and 50 meters wide), where they were formed into blocks – literally the building blocks of the ship, later to be assembled like a jigsaw puzzle into *QM2*.

On July 4, 2002 – 162 years to the day since Cunard's first ship, *Britannia*, set sail on her maiden voyage from Liverpool to North America – Cunard celebrated *QM2*'s keel laying, the spiritual if no longer literal birth of the new vessel. From the preassembly zone, the first blocks that would form the central bottom section of the hull, supporting the main engines, were lifted by Chantiers' immense gantry cranes and set down gently in the construction dock. Over the next 13 months, 97 more blocks would follow as *QM2* grew outward and upward, her engines installed, her upper decks laid in, and her structure gradually filled with wiring, ventilation, and plumbing. By November 2002, 49 of her

98 total blocks were on board. On February 4, 2003, her bridge block was lifted into position, and on March 12, the bottom section of her funnel followed – the final element to be installed before float-out. Her construction dock was filled with water, and on March 21, assisted by eight tugboats, *Queen Mary 2* set sail for the first time, traversing the short distance to her finishing dock at Chantiers' Basin C.

It was now bells-and-whistles time, as *QM2* ceased being just an engineering project and started putting on her face. Safety systems were checked, temporary lighting replaced, galleys equipped, décor installed, and trials of propulsion and electrical systems begun in preparation for her September sea trials. By late May, 1,000 of her 2,017 passenger and crew cabins had been installed (having been prebuilt nearby, brought to the berth by truck, and hoisted to their correct decks by huge external elevators), and 60

©Harvey Lloyd

master plasterers from Paris were at work on her public rooms' decorative ceilings. By June, painters began transforming her battleship-grey hull into classic liner black, applying nautical white to her superstructure, and banding her funnel in the traditional Cunard black and red. The finest fine-tuning also continued: If you were up before sunrise one morning, you might even have seen a bleary-eyed Gerry Ellis trekking to the other side of the Chantiers yard to determine which type of fiber optics best illuminated the name *Queen Mary 2* on the vessel's superstructure off in the distance.

There was still the matter of the whistle to go with all those bells. In mid-April 2003, the top section of *QM2*'s funnel was attached. Mounted on its starboard side, gleaming white and more than seven feet long, was one of the original midship whistles from the great *Queen Mary* – the same whistle that had sounded when she made her first crossing in 1936, and when she carried American soldiers home from war in 1945 celebrating victory. Refurbished by its original manufacturer, and sitting opposite an exact replica to port, that whistle is ready to once again blow its famous bass A note across the North Atlantic sea, linking Cunard's illustrious past to an equally illustrious future.

a new queen for a new generation

©Harvey Lloyd.

while the hull defines the shape of a liner, the inside is filled with the dreams and imagination of those who are responsible for marketing her.

From left to right: Deborah Natansohn, senior vice president of sales and marketing; Artist rendering of Canyon Ranch SpaClub; Artist rendering of Illuminations.

"We always said that if we could get new people to book the transatlantic, the rest would be easy," says Deborah Natansohn, Cunard senior vice president of sales and marketing, the creative force behind the rebranding of the line with *Queen Mary 2*. Faced with the challenge of filling the largest and grandest ship ever built, Natansohn early on found herself locked away for a week on *Queen Elizabeth 2* as part of the Cunard team charged with creating the ultimate ocean liner of the 21st century.

"We went through every element of the ship – from the dining to the entertainment to the spa to the cabin design – to determine what elements had to be there to attract a whole new generation to transatlantic travel."

It was a challenge the industry veteran faced with confidence. Today, with *QM2* sales far exceeding the line's most

optimistic expectations – the maiden voyage sold out in record time, and some 65 percent of the passengers booking are new to Cunard – Natansohn seems more than pleased with the way "the combination of product on board and our communication of it" has been working.

When the native New Yorker joined Cunard in November 2000, she brought a wealth of experience in marketing cruises and land tours, as well as executive management skills from her former position as president of Orient Lines, the only woman to hold such a job when she earned it in 1998. She has also chaired the marketing committee for the industry organization Cruise Line International Association (CLIA).

"Creatively, the marketing team has very much been part of what the product should be," says Natansohn, who was involved in every aspect of *QM2*, from choosing the china pattern and uniforms to approving the ship's décor. "We had a choice early on," she says. "We could have made the ship a faux retro liner, almost like a Hollywood rendition of a cruise liner, which looked like something from the past. But every Cunard ship had been a ship of its time, innovative and contemporary."

Decades ago, for example, Cunard ships were the first to offer electricity, and when *QE2* made her debut in the late 1960s, many of her furnishings and uniforms had a trendy, modern appeal.

"So we were creating a new product which certainly respected the historic traditions of Cunard, but we also had a very strong vision about what this new *Queen Mary 2* needed to be," says Natansohn. "We wanted to make it a 21st-century ship, with all the amenities that a sophisticated and experienced traveller would expect today, while maintaining the grandeur and grace of a classic ocean liner."

A New Market

A key element in the marketing strategy for the new liner was to target baby boomers. The company needed to overcome "a little bit of their old-fashioned image," to appear grand, with traditional service, but not stuffy. "We

wanted to feel a little more *hip*," Natansohn says.

Natansohn and her team researched the market and found that time also was a major consideration for many target passengers. The challenge was to entice them to take six days to do what they might accomplish in as many hours: to sail instead of fly across the Atlantic.

"Those six days would have to be considered time well spent," she says. "We had to make time the greatest gift that somebody could give themselves."

That might mean time spent enjoying pampering spa treatments or working out in the fitness centre, taking language or acting lessons or sitting in on seminars about art and architecture. It could also mean spending quality time with family, enjoying world-class cuisine, and even learning how to cook with a master chef.

"We set out to make the ship so rich in features that it was an attraction in itself, so much that people felt that six days weren't enough to do all that they wanted to do on board," says Natansohn.

Cunard veterans are well acquainted with the line's many amenities. To reach first-time Cunard cruisers, Natansohn set out to convey the level of luxury they could expect from a cruise aboard *QM2*.

From the beginning, Cunard pursued a strong co-branding policy to

promote the luxury aspect. The spa on *QM2* is not just any spa but the widely acclaimed Canyon Ranch SpaClub®. The new ship also boasts the first floating Veuve Clicquot Champagne Bar. Cuisine is world class and served on Wedgwood china with Waterford glassware. And lecturers are far from run of the mill; they hail from the University of Oxford and the Royal Academy of Dramatic Art.

"People buy a vacation because they want to fulfill their needs, not yours," Natansohn says. "That's why the approach we took for *QM2* was very much based on what the market told us were their interests."

Baby boomers, she says, tend to like options. That was an important part in planning dining venues on *QM2*. "We looked at all the various dining modes that had become vogue in the cruise industry. Alternative dining was hot, options a very big thing among the younger generation. They like choice."

Alternative dining options aboard *QM2* include restaurants specializing in Asian and Italian cuisines, a British carvery, and a Chef's Galley, where passengers can learn to cook what they eat on any given night.

"We'll still have the Queens Grill and the Princess Grill and the Golden Lion pub, but there are a lot of elements on *QM2* that we don't have on *QE2*, and we wanted to make sure we created them in a top-notch way. What you get at the Todd English restaurant on *QM2* is the same cuisine that you'd expect if you walked into his stateside restaurant."

Tradition and Choice

The new generation of cruisers also is more sophisticated about technology. "We invested quite a lot of money into a digital, interactive TV system that every cabin will have," Natansohn says. From the comfort of their quarters, passengers may send and receive e-mail, review and purchase shore excursions and photographs, order wine for dinner, watch dozens of movies, create a personalised music play list and even request that a light bulb be replaced.

"If there's one thing a deluxe passenger doesn't like to do it's to stand in queue," Natansohn says. The in-cabin TV system will cut down on crowding. "With a ship carrying 2,600 passengers, we had to be conscious of that."

So while there are plenty of traditional Cunard elements aboard *QM2* to attract the faithful – the Queens Room, with ballroom dancing; proper afternoon tea

served daily in several venues; British nannies to watch the children and a kennel to care for pets – the new ship will offer sufficient innovations to attract a new generation of cruisers Natansohn hopes will become the "newly faithful."

Some changes, Natansohn concedes, may not please everyone. For example, there is no smoking in the dining rooms, and shows feature jazzier, bigger revues. "But there are other places to smoke, and we'll still have classical music and theatrical performances in different venues of the ship. There will be so much going on simultaneously that there will always be something for everyone."

Ocean Books is back with the library and bookstore, which have been so popular. "But here's the change," adds Natansohn, "we'll also have books on CD." And don't overlook Cunard ConneXions, the largest space on any ship dedicated to education. *QM2* also boasts more elaborate sporting equipment as well as a more sophisticated children's center with computers.

Those familiar with *QE2*'s Heritage Trail will be pleased to find that they can also take a self-guided audio tour of *QM2*'s Maritime Quest (MQ), a museum-quality exhibit highlighting the line's rich history. The world's first shipboard planetarium features high-tech

presentations and virtual reality shows, with prominent astronomers on many of the voyages to explain the night sky.

And to take the place of the Concord is Cunard's "Ultimate *QM2* Vacation," pairing one of the ship's two top suites with one-way transatlantic air via private Gulfstream IV-SP jet. *QM2* is also seeking a broad range of passengers with various pricing levels and cruise lengths.

Whereas advertising for *QE2* over the last three years featured black-and-white photos of affluent passengers enjoying themselves on board a ship, *QM2*'s early ads featured women in evening gowns doing mundane tasks while dreaming of a voyage on the new ship. "More often in marketing," says Natansohn, "the market itself lets you know when it's time for a

change." Because women tend to make family vacation decisions, the successful "Can you wait?" advertising campaign was designed to appeal especially to them.

"But while advertising starts creating the image for you and creates anticipation" says Natansohn, "it's the on-board product and word of mouth that are critically important. That's why it is so important we give our clients, especially in the first year, an absolutely fabulous experience, so that word of mouth will independently confirm what we promise."

Every ship has its own soul, Natansohn believes. "It takes time to ripen it, but *QM2* will develop its own character, and it will certainly be rooted in the British heritage and tradition of Cunard."

Simmons

would like to congratulate

Cunard on the launch of

the Queen Mary 2.

We are excited to provide you with a first class mattress
designed especially for Cunard.

Simmons is dedicated to pampering you by bringing you Better Sleep
Through Science®. Our special collection of soft covers and comforting
foam is engineered to ensure a great night's rest while on your cruise.
Simmons® Beautyrest® mattress is designed so you feel less of your partner's
movement, giving you the royal treatment every night. After enjoying the
comfort of a plush Simmons® mattress during your cruise, why not sleep
on the best all year round? Bring luxury to everyday living with a
Simmons® Beautyrest® mattress.

Enjoy Simmons® Beautyrest® With Cunard And at Home!

Lunn Poly

Promoting excellence in cruising

At Lunn Poly we are dedicated to finding the perfect cruise for you.
We have more than 250 cruise specialists nationwide offering;

- Huge choice of cruises
- Expert advice
- Great deals

We promise to beat anyone on price on any cruise holiday

✎ **Click** lunnpoly.com

☎ **Call 0870 162 5671** Open late

🚶 **Come in** Shops nationwide, many open Sunday

World of TUI

It seems like only yesterday I was on the voyage of a lifetime . . .

Suddenly, she's no longer in her cubicle, she's back under the Caribbean sun.

Cruise memories can brighten any day, and at Image, our business is capturing

memorable moments. There are good reasons why Image is the largest and fastest-

growing shipboard photography concessionaire in the industry - service, quality, innovation.

IMAGE
Service ~ Quality ~ Innovation

Contact Brynley Davies
Image, P.O. Box 448, Grand Cayman, BWI; vox: 345-945-3737, fax: 345-945-3782 / Image Photo Services, 5040 NW 7th Street, Suite 250, Miami FL 33126; vox: 305-476-3666, fax: 305-476-3663

Special Cruises...

...at Special Prices

"and that's a promise."

Philip Nuttall
Managing Director

...For Early Booking Savings or Those Last Minute Decisions...

Just another day in paradise!

THE WEST INDIAN COMPANY, LTD.

PROUD TO WELCOME YOU TO HAVENSIGHT, ST. THOMAS.

the reality

"A musician must make music, an artist must paint, a poet must write, if he is to be ultimately at peace with himself. What a man can be, he must be."

–Abraham Harold Maslow

the art of cruising

Ken Kast

"Australia" by Christianson Lee Studios.

dozens of artists and designers have produced original
works to grace the new *Queen Mary 2.*

From left to right:
"England by the Sea" by
Charles Bourke Wildbank;
"Southern Hemisphere" by
Christianson Lee Studios;
"Asia" by Christianson Lee Studios.

How do you decorate the largest, longest, tallest, most expensive passenger ship ever built? If you're art historian Erik Hermida, the answer is: very carefully.

Cunard Line commissioned Hermida, director of Enterprise & Art, to supply the 150,000-ton *Queen Mary 2* with a wealth of original creations, including sculptures, paintings, murals, relief panels, mosaics, and integrated art forms.

To find the perfect complements to the ship, Hermida consulted with dozens of artists, designers, and architects from the around the world. He ended up commissioning 128 artists from 16 countries to create 565 original works. Among the creative contributors are 30 British artists who came up with more than 100 original pieces for staterooms, many printed and signed by the artist.

"It's not rocket science," Hermida concedes, "but there are a lot of difficulties in hanging a piece of art on a cruise ship rather than in art gallery."

For starters, there are fire regulations to consider. Art on a cruise ship must not be flammable. Thus, paintings on the new ship have been done on lightweight aluminum, not on canvas.

Then there are aesthetic challenges. *QM2* has been designed to reflect the style and graciousness of an earlier era. "She's a long, elegant liner, not a big, bulky cruise ship," as Hermida says. "The art needs to reflect that."

Some cruise lines, he says, cut corners, encouraging artists to use inferior or faux materials. "That's very Las Vegas," Hermida says. "We tried to stay away from that as much as we could."

As a result, there are real marble statues in *QM2*'s health spa; authentic bronze statues in the Grand Lobby, Queens Grill, and Princess Grill; and a 24-foot-long genuine marble table inlaid

with multicoloured semi-precious stones in the Royal Court.

Hermida also overlooked no details in the Winter Garden on Deck 7. Here British artist and muralist Ian Cairnie has created a 60-foot x 25-foot *trompe l'oeil* ceiling that resembles a garden full of lush verdure and birds.

"The whole idea of the Winter Garden is that you're in a big country house surrounded by tropical plants," Hermida explains. "The walls are decorated with panels that look through cast iron outside to an airbrushed landscape with rolling hills, deer, and houses."

Seafaring Style

Cairnie also created a wall in the Empire Casino that evokes the elegant ambiance of Monaco gaming. The work of American artist Charles Wildbank, on the other hand, is featured above the stairs to the aft promenades. As a child who could not speak or hear, Wildbank began drawing pictures – candy, fruit, cake, soda – to communicate his wants. His attempts to communicate evolved into a noteworthy career as an artist. For *QM2*, Wildbank produced two large British and American landscapes.

Much of the art on the new ship pays homage to the original *Queen Mary*. Scottish sculptor John McKenna created a modern interpretation of a 1930s relief that graced the first ship. McKenna's version is a 450-square-foot bronze panel that depicts *QM2* on her transatlantic route.

For the Princess and Queens grills, U.S. photographer Andrew Bordwin offers up an array of shots featuring stylish Art Deco buildings. "This conveys a sense of the grand age of liners, without exactly copying it," says Hermida. "It refers to the Art Deco style of *Queen Mary*, but

From left to right: "Spring" by DKT;
Floral paintings in the Britannia
restaurant by Martin van Vreden;
"Combat" by Andrew Bordwin.

uses modern photography." Adding to the ambiance in each Grill are two life-size bronze statues depicting abstract interpretations of the female form.

Textiles also play an important role in decorating *QM2*. A 300-square-foot Gobelin-style tapestry by Dutch textile artist Barbara Broekman hangs in the Britannia restaurant. The scene depicts *QM2* against the New York skyline, replete with streamers waving through the slats of the Brooklyn Bridge.

The walls of the 20,000-square-foot Canyon Ranch SpaClub are decorated with 11 small carpets and one large one. The pieces are all woven and dyed by hand and stretched over aluminum frames. Instead of combustible natural fibers, British weaver Ptolemy Mann used safe synthetic fibers called Trevira.

Like those of its famous predecessor, the walls of central walkways on *QM2* are adorned with decorations of *verre*

eglomise (black painted glass) and carved and etched glass.

"Most ships have a wraparound promenade," says Hermida. "This one has a path, a main street, in the middle, so you see outside. The walkway is lavishly decorated in a modern, updated version of Art Deco." The panels depict the northern and southern hemispheres in gold, silver, and deep red. As you walk through the space, the light appears to change.

Two life-size glass dresses by Dutch designer Patula Berm hang at the entrance of the Royal Court Theatre. One dress is covered with gold stars and silver leaf; the other is multicoloured, multilayered, and decorated with various pieces of colored glass.

Everywhere you look aboard *QM2*, your eyes are treated to aesthetic delights.

"The place is full of art," Hermida says. "It's very special and unique."

dining in style

from celebrity chefs to innovative entrées, *QM2* offers guests an unforgettable adventure in food.

From left to right:
Daniel Boulud;
Todd English

Oscar Wilde quipped that he could resist everything but temptation. When it comes to food, diners aboard the *Queen Mary 2* are tempted at every turn. But why resist? The culinary offerings on this stylish liner simply aren't to be missed.

"We're trying to do it a bit differently than ever before," says Karl Muhlberger, corporate executive chef. "We're going for different concepts."

The liner also is going for dining diversity. There are 10 – count 'em, 10 – dining establishments on *QM2*. The main dining room is the 1,300-seat Britannia restaurant, which offers open seating for breakfast and lunch and two nightly seatings for dinner. Among the entrées that will make your mouth water are roasted beef fillet with whiskey sauce and Belgian endive, and tournedos soufflé with fondant potato and foie gras sauce.

Guests staying in suites and junior suites are welcome at the upscale Queens

Grill and Princess Grill. The Queens Grill accommodates 200 and features succulent appetisers such as poached prawns on citrus salad with crispy Thai ginger pork skin, and steamed lobster with tomato and basil jelly. The Princess Grill serves international fare, including Mexican-, Portuguese-, and Chinese-inspired specialties, such as Oriental pork medallions with basmati rice.

"We try to be authentic and be true to the culture," says Muhlberger. "A Greek salad features ingredients that they'd use in Greece."

The Kings Court (referred to as the Lido on many other ships) is open for breakfast and lunch, with a 24-hour section featuring pizza, pannini, a salad bar, and rich desserts made on board. On the upper deck, there's an outdoor café for lighter fare.

Stars shine brightly in *QM2*'s culinary family. French-born Daniel Boulud – whose

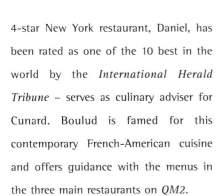

4-star New York restaurant, Daniel, has been rated as one of the 10 best in the world by the *International Herald Tribune* – serves as culinary adviser for Cunard. Boulud is famed for this contemporary French-American cuisine and offers guidance with the menus in the three main restaurants on *QM2*.

"We're thrilled that a chef as renowned as Daniel is overseeing the creation of our menus," says Deborah L. Natansohn, senior vice president of sales and marketing for Cunard.

"It's an honor for me," adds Boulud.

Another Helping

In addition, acclaimed restaurateur and TV personality Todd English is the creative force behind an innovative *QM2* restaurant called, appropriately enough, Todd English.

Named one of *People* magazine's "50 Most Beautiful People," English gained

fame with Olives, his first restaurant in Charlestown, Massachusetts, which *Esquire* magazine has added to its "Top 10 Restaurants" list. In addition, English was *Bon Appetit's* "Restaurateur of the Year" in 2001.

In his new *QM2* restaurant, English has overlooked no details. "Todd has developed the room, chosen the china, the uniforms, the whole thing," says Muhlberger.

"It's a challenge and also a great honor," says English, whose 156-seat restaurant highlights Mediterranean cuisine. "Being involved with *Queen Mary 2* is very exciting for me."

Want to learn to cook like a master yourself? Stop by the Chef's Galley in Kings Court. Here, guest chefs will teach you how to prepare meals that are mouthwatering just before you dine on the creation. The galley features a mirrored work station, so you won't miss

a trick as your teacher slices, dices, and juliennes.

For breakfast and lunch, Kings Court features casual dining in an open pavilion. At night, the space is transformed with dividers into four sit-down eateries, each with its own china, menus, wine lists, and server uniforms.

In addition to the Chef's Galley, there's the 210-seat Lotus, which serves Chinese, Thai, Japanese, and Indian fare, including Oriental spiced crab cake, coconut with roasted peanuts and red chili dip, steamed skin-roasted sea bass on spring greens, and vanilla-scented foam. La Piazza, which has 66 seats, serves pastas,

pizza, and other Italian delicacies, such as spaghetti puttanesca in a braised plum tomato sauce with black olives, capers, and oregano. At The Carvery, a 160-seat ode to Cunard's British heritage, you can enjoy succulent slices of beef, lamb, pork, and poultry. Consider prime rib of beef, Yorkshire pudding, roasted potatoes, braised baby cabbage, and glazed carrots.

Watching your weight? Don't worry. Canyon Ranch has integrated its spa

cuisine into the daily menu, listing the calories and fat content of selections. And if you prefer to eat in the privacy of your own room, you can order hot and cold items from room service 24 hours a day.

Of course, none of this means much if the food isn't presented beautifully, but naturally, that's also been taken care of. Wedgwood has designed more than 90,000 pieces of porcelain and glassware for assorted venues on the ship, including the Queens Grill and the Princess Grill. The signature *QM2* table setting is made from Connaught bone china decorated with borders of platinum and gold; some items also feature the Cunard logo in gold. Various pieces are also available in the ship's boutique, so you can even take a little bit of your vacation dining experience home with you.

"We have a fine tradition and our expectations are high," Muhlberger says. "These are our guests' expectations, too, and we aim to deliver."

let us entertain you

finding ways to fill your days is not a problem on *QM2*, from 30 simulated golf courses to the most spectacular shows between New York and London.

Aboard *Queen Mary 2*, your toughest decision will be how to spend your time – and there are countless entertainment options from which to choose.

Are you a golf fanatic? There's a game with your name on it. Hit the putting green right on deck. Prefer to cuddle up with a good book? There's a library stocked with everything from Phil Roth to Dr. Phil. Could you spend hours gazing up at the stars? The first planetarium ever built on a ship is on *QM2*.

Maybe you'd rather just sit back and let others entertain you. For movie mavens, *QM2* offers a theatre with the latest and greatest. Want to try your hand at blackjack? You're in luck. Just head for the Empire Casino. Cabaret? You got it. The largest ballroom at sea, the Queens Room, also is on *QM2*, so you can perfect your Cha Cha or learn to Rumba. You can even drop by the computer and surf the Web as you're, ahem, surfing the waves.

"We want to offer passengers lots of different choices," says Martin Lilly, Cunard's director of entertainment. "We see the ship as a small city and feel that the entertainment should reflect that ambiance."

What makes a great night in the city? You might enjoy dinner at a fine restaurant, then sit down to a good show. "Diversity," Lilly says. "That's what we're trying to achieve."

And by all accounts, it's working. There are nine entertainment venues on *QM2*, including the Commodore Club for jazz; the Golden Lion for a traditional pub atmosphere; G32, a nightclub featuring a variety of worldwide music; and the Royal Court Theatre, featuring the most spectacular new shows between New York and London. *Rock @ the Opera* fuses the drama and excellence of opera with the excitement of contemporary rock music; *Zing Went the Strings* is an affectionate tribute to the songs, films, shows, and life

of one of the most adored divas of our time – Judy Garland; and *Apassionata* is an extravaganza of exciting styles and cultures of dance from around the world.

In addition, there are cabaret shows in the Queens Room. "So you might get in an early show there and then head on to the Royal Court Theatre," says Lilly. "Later you can take in a planetarium show or a movie."

Or go to a bar – another staple of urban nightlife. But on this ship you won't find just any old pub. On *QM2* you'll find the only Veuve Clicquot Champagne Bar at sea, a 64-seat venue in the fashionable Mayfair Shops area of the ship. The Veuve Clicquot Bar features a variety of champagnes as well as a menu including caviar and *foie gras*.

As you may know, Clicquot is one of the oldest and most prestigious producers of champagne, sold in more than 120 countries. Philippe Clicquot founded the house in 1772. The motto: "Only one quality ... the finest" remains the foundation on which the company rests.

"Veuve Clicquot has a rich history and tradition of offering the very finest quality to its patrons," said Deborah Natansohn, senior vice president of sales and marketing for Cunard Line. "We're thrilled that *Queen Mary 2* will add to her list of 'firsts,' a shipboard Veuve Clicquot Champagne Bar."

Be a Star

But entertainment doesn't have to be passive, Lilly maintains. "I'm very keen that a lot of the entertainment we offer is active, so passengers can participate."

On *QM2,* you can jump right in and learn while you're having fun. Cunard ConneXions – workshops, seminars, and lectures conducted by professors, historians, scientists, and other experts – features cooking classes, wine appreciation sessions, foreign language classes, and photography workshops. There's even a University of Oxford programme, highlighting lectures from some of Britain's brightest minds. These are held in the 10,225-square-foot learning space, which is composed of seven classrooms and an auditorium.

The "Oxford Discovery" series offers courses on subjects such as "British and American Music" and "Culture of the 1960s," "Shakespeare on Film," "Modern Art from the Tate to the Met," and "The Internet Explosion." (Speaking of the 'Net, you can view the course list on Cunard's Web site at least 90 days prior to departure.)

"A *QM2* transatlantic crossing gives you the luxury of time to pursue interests that you always put on the back burner at home," says Natansohn.

Architectural Digest magazine's "Designing the Seas" series, also part of

Cunard ConneXions, just might inspire you to overhaul your home. Top architects and interior designers present on-board lectures and offer private one-on-one design consultations with passengers. The designers – many of whom have also graced the magazine's coveted list of "The World's Top 100 Designers" – help you to know more about building a collection, architectural history, displaying fine artwork, and historic gardens.

The *Architectural Digest* collection of architects and designers is published up to six months in advance of the voyage on the Datebook pages of the magazine and posted on its ArchDigest.com web site. A listing also is at Cunard.com.

But the *piece de resistance* is a chance to study with members of the London-based Royal Academy of Dramatic Art. "With the RADA programme," Lilly says, "passengers can watch a play one day and the following day they can join in a play reading or be directed by one of the senior actors from the troupe."

RADA students have included Sir John Gielgud, Vivien Leigh, Sir Anthony

May you enjoy smooth sailing, a joyful heart

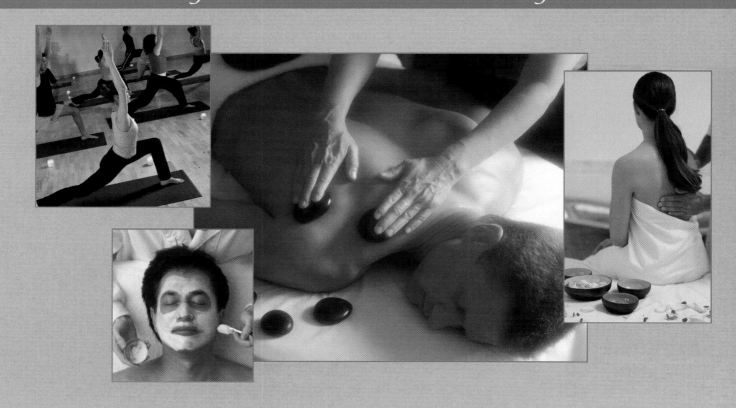

Hopkins, Joan Collins, Peter O'Toole, Kenneth Branagh, and Ralph Fiennes. Now you can add your name to this prestigious list.

Under the Cunard Repertory Programme, Academy members will be on *QM2* about 40 weeks a year, performing and sharing secrets of their craft with passengers. The main presentation – a Shakespearean tragedy, perhaps, or the latest offering from Tom Stoppard – will be offered twice on transatlantic crossings; on longer runs, the cast will perform each evening and offer acting workshops during the day.

"We are very pleased that RADA students will have the opportunity to perform on the extraordinary new *Queen Mary 2* and to share their love of theatre with Cunard's international clientele," says Antonia Gillum-Webb, chief executive of RADA Enterprises, Ltd., the academy's commercial subsidiary.

Whether you're watching a play or performing in one, you're sure to have the time of your life on a *QM2* cruise. When it comes to entertainment on this stylish liner, every passenger is a star.

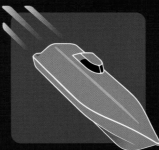

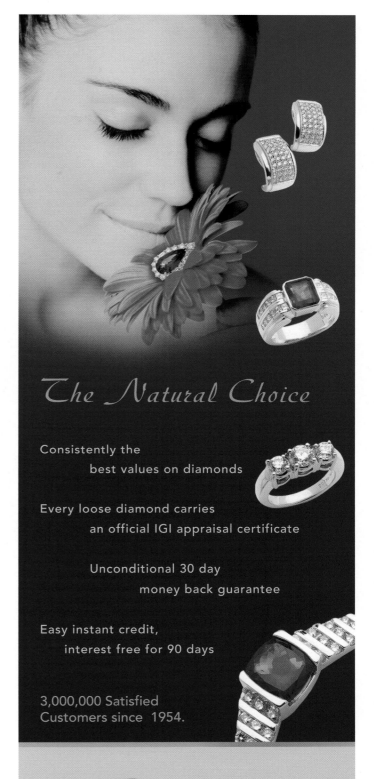

the glory

*"Tomorrow once
again we sail
the Ocean Sea."*

–Quintus Horatius Flaccus

reviving the glory days of cruising

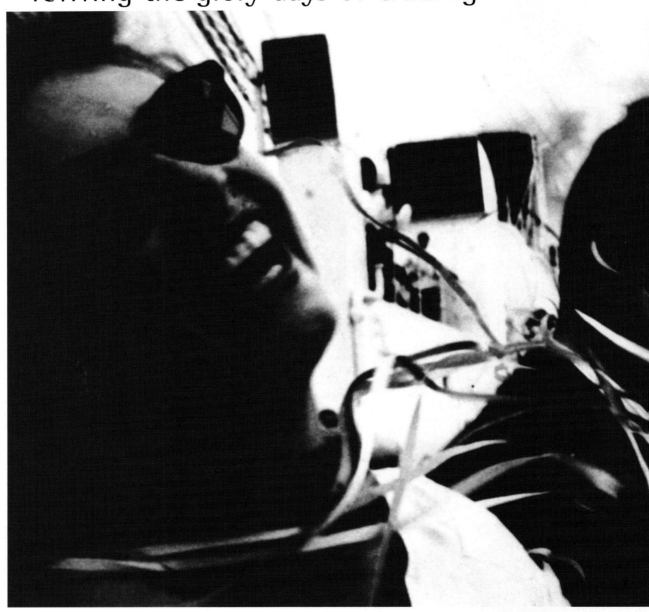

the new *Queen Mary 2* ushers in a renaissance
in elegant, stylish cruising.

In an era of mobile phones, space shuttles, Internet communication, and 24-hour television, can a new ocean liner recapture the glory days of cruising, when the world seemed to turn at a slower, gentler pace?

That is the issue facing Cunard Line, whose new *Queen Mary 2* attempts to redefine the essence of sea travel, offering the style and grace of yesteryear in the rapidly evolving marketplace of the 21st century.

Certainly the mechanics of shipbuilding have advanced in quantum bounds since the 1930s, when workers embedded some 10 million rivets in the hull of the original *Queen Mary*. So, too, have the wants and needs of passengers changed.

The task for *Queen Mary 2* is to offer modern cruisers the best qualities of Then and Now. But how? What do we envision when we seek to revive cruising's glory days? What are the elements required to rekindle that mythical quality that is so alluring yet so hard to define?

Cruising has become a much more enticing vacation option in recent years, but that old-time elegance, that sense of heritage and tradition is lacking on most modern cruise ships. Beauty, as they say, is only skin deep, and too often glitter and glitz are mistaken for glamour.

To revive the glory days, the new *QM2* must have an air of refinement and sophistication that transcends the ambiance of other ships. She must eschew the obvious in favor of the subtle, offer glamour without resorting to glitz. She must evoke the grandeur of the past while offering all of the amenities of the modern age. She must be an individual, a leader, an innovator.

Reviving the glory days is not simply a matter of recreating the past. Any line could do that. The task for Cunard is to bring back that old sense of style and

elegance while also offering the brightest of technological amenities.

QM2's architects and designers could not duplicate existing blueprints or copy recent newbuilds. This is a new ballgame, but the rules span a century. Designers thus had to keep an eye on yesterday as they endeavoured to produce a masterpiece for today.

When it came to technology, there could be no turning back the clock. Only the most advanced tools could be employed to produce a ship like *QM2*. Nor could Cunard overlook the expectations and requirements of contemporary passengers.

A New Age of Style

Some attributes of earlier liners simply no longer are appropriate. At one time the primary function of a liner was to transport passengers across an ocean. Passengers today no longer undertake voyages to get from one port to another. The ease and frequency of air travel has diminished that need.

Vast areas of open deck space are no longer *de rigueur*, the inside promenade has been ruled obsolete, and swimming pools need not be hidden away in the bowels of a vessel. Cabins, for the vast majority of passengers, are not seen as fundamentally functional, but rather as sumptuous, comfortable spaces to enjoy. And certainly entertainment is far more varied and complex today than in decades past.

Cunard architects and designers had to take a different tack in several areas. Instead of expansive open decks, there are outdoor bars, sports courts, golf course simulators, health spas, theatres, and large, inviting pools. Instead of serried ranks of portholes stretching up from the waterline, a ship must new offer a large number of cabins with balconies. And while an old-time liner might offer

only a ballroom, smoking lounge, card room, gymnasium, and library, a 21st-century vessel must provide passengers with many more leisure options and activities. Dining preferences, too, are vastly different today. The accent now is on alternative restaurants, more healthy fare, and round-the-clock options.

Reviving the glory days, then, is a formidable task. But Cunard is a company that stays in touch with the past while looking to the future. With that philosophy in mind, the line has employed ultramodern technology while honouring tradition. That is most evident in the yard chosen to build *QM2*.

France's historic Chantiers de l'Atlantique enjoys a rich heritage and a reputation for quality work. The scope of the talents brought to bear on our modern has evolved from the workmanship that gave birth to such legends as *Normandie*, *Ile de France*, and *SS France*. At this yard is a dedicated group of workers versed in the technical know-how of today, yet mindful of the traditions of yesterday.

DUPLEX APARTMENTS

Under that careful stewardship, *QM2* has grown from a seemingly impossible dream to a firm reality. She is a modern classic, displaying the attributes of a breed once considered by some to have become extinct. She offers understated charm and elegance, an appeal that crosses cultural differences. The new *Queen Mary 2* is a magnificent achievement for our times and a glorious tribute to a glorious age of cruising.

Long may her legend live on.

Arist rendering of the Commodore Club.

have a nice trip!

Port of Piraeus
the nearby port to any destination

PIRAEUS PORT AUTHORITY sa
Leading Mediterranean port

PIRAEUS PORT AUTHORITY SA • 10 Akti Miaouli Str, GR 185 38 Piraeus - Greece
tel: ++30210.4520911 -17 • fax: ++30210.4286843
internet site: www.olp.gr • e-mail: olpdsx@otenet.gr

Hemisphere is proud to be associated
with the launch of the magnificent

We wish her well as she joins
the world's most famous
ocean liners, continuing
Cunard's unrivalled
tradition of luxury cruising
long into the 21st century.

QUEEN MARY 2

DESIGN • ADVERTISING • MARKETING

Ten Barley Mow Passage Tel +44 (0)20 8742 2533 www.hemisphere-design.co.uk
London W4 4PH Fax +44 (0)20 8742 2536 London • Florida

Laundries made to measure.

Tech Marine provides high quality laundries and laundromats on a turn-key basis and ensures that every detail is covered before and during installation.

Outfitting and managing hotel service areas on large passenger cruise vessels are not easy tasks. Planning is the key.

Thanks to years of qualified experience in working closely with prestigious customers, **Tech Marine** has the know-how in the marine engineering field to solve any problem.

Through innovation and the search for excellence, **Tech Marine** has put together a wide range of hi-tech machinery with proven suitability in the marine environment.

We are always ready to work with our customers on new and fresh ideas to ensure the best outfitting and installation solutions. We guarantee our results, which are proven on over 60 vessels!

TECH MARINE S.p.A.
www.techmarine.it

UDINE (Italy)
V.le Palmanova, 73/R - 33100
tel: +39 0432 528511   fax: +39 0432 528512
sales@techmarine.it

SAINT NAZAIRE (France)
Bd des Apprentis, B.P. 6 - 44601
tel: +33 2 40 22 69 33   fax: +33 2 40 22 65 21
techmarine.france@wanadoo.fr

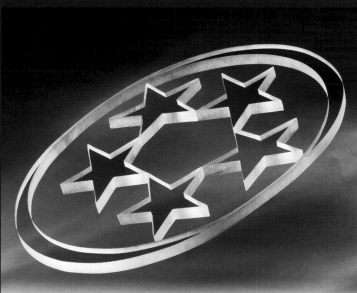

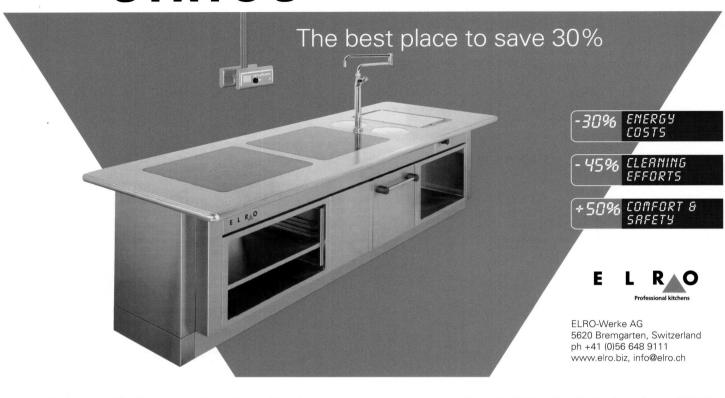

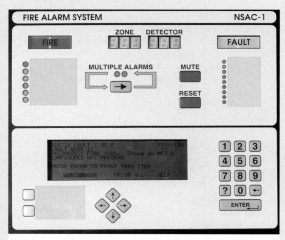

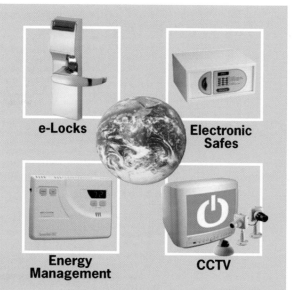

advertiser index

special thanks to Harvey Lloyd

Queen Mary 2 The Greatest Ocean Liner of Our Time. Photographs by Harvey Lloyd. Text by John Maxtone-Graham. In January 2004, Cunard Line's latest flagship, the *Queen Mary 2*, will sail on her maiden voyage from England. This fourth Cunard Queen is a true ocean liner, able to cross the Atlantic in all weathers at high speed, expanding Cunard's celebrated heritage. Carpe Diem Books is producing a major coffee-table book, *Queen Mary 2: The Greatest Ocean Liner of Our Time*, for Bulfinch Press /AOL Time Warner Books. The book documents the creation of this remarkable vessel from keel laying to christening. Scheduled for publication in April 2004, it features stunning four-color photographs by the world-renowned photographer and digital artist Harvey Lloyd. The images include details of design, construction, engines, lavish interiors and decks, exquisite shipboard art, and the sea trials and christening. The book also contains archival images of *Queen Mary 2*'s historic predecessors. An eight-page gatefold shows a detailed cutaway of the remarkable interiors. The publication date will coincide with the first historic encounter of QE2 and QM2 in New York harbor. QM2 is a record-breaker. Four city blocks long and as tall as the Statue of Liberty, at $800-million, she is the largest, most luxurious and most expensive passenger vessel of all time. Her public rooms include a planetarium, ballroom, theatre, cinema, Canyon Ranch Spa and ten restaurants. Twenty-six hundred passengers will be accommodated in a splendid variety of suites and cabins, three-quarters of them with balconies overlooking the sea. Harvey Lloyd is a seasoned adventure travel and aerial photographer and artist and the foremost photographer of the cruise industry today. His most recent book is *Voyages, The Romance of Cruising* (Dorling Kindersley, 1999). John Maxtone-Graham is a world-renowned maritime historian and the author of more than a dozen books about passenger vessels.

BRITISH AIRWAYS
Preferred Partner

Travelling Companions

Whether on the ground or in the air, British Airways always sets itself the highest standards.
We continue this tradition through our partnership with Cunard. Flying to over 250 destinations,
with a choice of four cabins on longhaul flights, your holiday is sure to start or finish in style.

FIRST

Check-in at dedicated FIRST desks before proceeding into the calm of the lounge

Exclusive 'demi-cabin' space creates a private environment

Each seat converts into a 6' 6" horizontal bed at the touch of a button

Fold down companion seat allows you to dine or chat with fellow FIRST passengers

Personal video player with a choice of 30 videos and 18 further video channels

A la Carte dining served with the finest wines and champagnes at a time convenient to you

Access to Arrivals lounge at Heathrow, Gatwick and Johannesburg airports

CLUB WORLD

Check-in at dedicated desks before proceeding into the lounge

Armchair style seat and footstool converts into a 6' fully flat bed at the touch of a button. Available on most routes. Other services offer the Cradle Seat with 4-way lumbar support*

Retractable privacy screens between seats on flights with flat beds

Personal video screen with 18 video channels

Sumptuous four course meal or delicious snacks served at a time convenient to you

Access to Arrivals lounge at Heathrow, Gatwick and Johannesburg airports

*Please check at time of booking.

WORLD TRAVELLER PLUS

A separate premier economy cabin with a maximum of five rows of seats

A wider seat than World Traveller with a 38" seat pitch, additional recline, adjustable lumbar support, head, leg and foot rests.

Seatback video screens offering 18 channels of continuous entertainment plus interactive games*

Three course meal and complimentary bar throughout the flight

In-seat phone and laptop power point

Skyflyer Disney activity packs to keep children occupied and a 'Kids Eat First' policy on pre-ordered children's meals

World Traveller Plus is being introduced across the network and is now available on most flights.

* Available on most aircraft.